Struggling with Israel
in a Marriage

Struggling with Israel
in a Marriage

Gina Crandell & David Roochnik

RESOURCE *Publications* · Eugene, Oregon

STRUGGLING WITH ISRAEL IN A MARRIAGE

Resource Publications
An Imprint of Wipf and Stock Publishers
199 W. 8th Ave., Suite 3
Eugene, OR 97401

www.wipfandstock.com

PAPERBACK ISBN: 979-8-3852-6198-7
HARDCOVER ISBN: 979-8-3852-6199-4
EBOOK ISBN: 979-8-3852-6200-7

VERSION NUMBER 092525

Preface

FOR MANY YEARS WE have discussed Israel-Palestine, and it's been a struggle. At our best, we listen to, and try to understand, each other. At our worst, we clam up and go our separate ways. Somewhere in-between are the many times we have argued and even screamed. We are both writers—more precisely, we are professors who have written a lot—and so, about a year ago, we decided we would each try to articulate not just our views about Israel-Palestine, but how these views changed over time. The next step was to merge our two stories into one. This short book is the result of that effort. It consists of an alternating sequence of sections in which first Gina, and then David, is the author. With a few exceptions it follows a chronological order. It begins with our childhoods and ends in the present. In selecting what memories to recount, we followed a simple rule: include only those that shaped our thinking about Judaism and Israel-Palestine.

Both of us have, naturally enough, been strongly influenced by books we've read, films we've seen, and websites we have consulted. We cite their titles and authors but provide no footnotes or hyperlinks. This is not an academic treatise. It is a coupling of the personal stories of two people who have long been deeply concerned about the violence and suffering that, for the past century, has plagued that tortured land between the River and the Sea.

Gina

IN JUNE 2024, A colleague of mine from a local climate activist group, who I knew mostly from Zoom meetings, took me aside at Springfest, a Town-wide event that calls for environmental action. She told me she'd read a letter of mine, which must have been published in the *Boston Globe* or *Brookline News,* and on the basis of that, she accused me of being an antisemite. I write many letters and more than one have voiced my strong opposition to Israel's massacre of Palestinians in Gaza and the U.S. support of it. So I wasn't sure to which she was referring. Perhaps I should have reminded this climate activist that the war had also generated a horrifying amount of planet-warming emissions. But I didn't. Instead I asked her if she knew that the Palestinians had been subjected to brutal violence since 1948. She responded by calling me a know-it-all and walking away.

I was shaken by this. Ever since I began expressing my opposition to the Israeli occupation of Palestine, I have wondered, when I have been called an antisemite, whether I actually am an antisemite or whether this term is primarily operating as a threat to scare people from criticizing Israel. Without a doubt, I hate what Israel is doing and I am furious at those American Jewish organizations who relentlessly lobby our government to support it. By what definition does that make me an antisemite?

David

I ARRIVED AT KIBBUTZ Kfar HaNassi in northern Israel in the Fall of 1971, and I liked it right away. The Galil, as the area is called, is beautiful, with rolling hills, planted fields, and Mount Hermon looming in the distance. The hard physical work I did in the citrus grove suited me. I enjoyed living in a cabin with the other volunteers, a good many of whom were neither American nor Jewish, and eating wholesome food in the cafeteria with all the kibbutzniks. I was glad to be outdoors most of every day and not to have to deal with money at all. Since Kfar HaNassi had been founded by immigrants from Great Britain, English was the first language of the older folks, and I was able to get to know several pretty well. I particularly admired Jason, the strong, capable, quiet man who was my boss in the citrus grove.

I have lots of good memories of my time in Israel, but three are especially vivid. First, a meeting was called by Ruth, the middle-aged woman who was in charge of us volunteers. She was prattling on about the rules and how things worked on the Kibbutz, when she gazed out the window and fell silent. It was twilight and especially gorgeous. Then, out of nowhere, she began to describe how astonishing it was that, after centuries of exile, the Jews had returned to Israel, and now here she was, born and raised in England but living on the same land as her ancestors, at home at last. To my amazement, she teared up. No longer a mousey clerk, she was having a mystical experience before my eyes, and it had been triggered by her vision of the land. She was awe-struck at being part of it, at being Jewish.

Although I had grown up in a largely Jewish milieu in New Jersey, Ruth's visceral identification with Israel was new to me. I took being Jewish as an inconsequential matter of fact, and it played little role in my experience of the world. My family belonged to a reformed congregation, but we only went to synagogue on the high holidays, an experience I found excruciating, and for Bar Mitzvahs. Both my parents were left-wing activists, and the strongest sense of identification they felt was not to their fellow Jews but to the working class. My mother wrote her own version of the Passover Haggadah, but it was mostly about our hope for the freedom of black Americans.

My family didn't talk much about Israel. Instead, our dinner table was dominated by my father's lectures about the War in Vietnam. I remember him ranting against the Tonkin Gulf Resolution of 1964, which authorized the President to use military force in Vietnam, and praising Wayne Morse, one of only two Senators to vote against it.

As a high-school student I followed in my parents' footsteps and regularly went to Central Park to protest against the War. During my first week of college in September of 1969, I joined the campus chapter of Students for a Democratic Society and resumed my anti-war activity. This blossomed into my full blown initiation into what was then called the "counterculture."

I did not go to Israel in 1971 because I felt any sense of belonging to an ancestral homeland. I went because, having dropped out of college after my sophomore year, I wanted to join the throngs of long-haired boys and girls who were wandering the world, and I'd heard a kibbutz was a good first stop on the hippy version of the grand tour. I hoped to join a caravan and travel to Iran or Afghanistan, or maybe Nepal . . . places I knew absolutely nothing about. Sure enough, that winter I was invited to join two English guys who were headed to India. At first I agreed, but I quickly realized I wasn't the traveler I thought, and maybe hoped, I was. I preferred the steady rhythms of daily life and hard work on Kfar HaNassi, and didn't want to leave.

My second memory is of a trip the Kibbutz organized to the Sinai Desert. Four years earlier, the Israeli Defense Force (IDF) had defeated the Egyptian army there, and dozens of wrecked tanks were strewn on that barren moonscape like dinosaur carcasses. We were in some sort of open vehicle—the rear of a truck, maybe—and I remember Jason gazing spellbound and nearly gasping. Was he amazed and proud of his country's triumph, or horrified by the carnage? Had he fought in the Sinai? Did he know men who died there? I had no idea what he was thinking.

My third memory is of my visit to Jerusalem. I was on my own, taking a holiday from the Kibbutz for a few days. I remember next to nothing about the Wailing Wall or the Temple Mount, or any of the other religious sites. No, what has stayed with me all these years is how pleasant, safe and welcoming the ancient city felt. The Palestinians were friendly and I came to love the simple meals of hummus, olives and pita bread I ate in their restaurants.

As much as I appreciated my time on the Kibbutz, and as much I was impressed by kibbutzniks like Ruth and Jason, I was not tempted to stay. For what I wanted was to return to school. During the rainy winter in the Galil, without a TV in sight and nowhere to go, I had read a lot and done some writing. I wanted to do more. I left Israel in May of 1972, and haven't been back since.

In 1973, my younger brother also lived on a kibbutz, but his experience was different. My stay at Kfar HaNassi came during a dream-like interlude of peace when there seemed to be hope on both sides. By contrast, my brother spent a lot of his time in bomb shelters during the Yom Kippur war that Israel came close to losing.

Gina

I DON'T SEE HOW I could have been antisemitic when I was a young child. I didn't know the word. Nor was I aware of knowing anyone who was Jewish. I can remember family members making "jokes" about how Catholics could sin and then get off scot free just by confessing. But I don't recall Jews ever being mentioned. Years later this led me to ask myself: Why isn't there a name for contemptuous speech about religions other than Judaism? Anti-Catholicism? Anti-Buddhism? What has made the word "anti-semitism" so exceptional?

My earliest recollection of knowing someone Jewish is a family I babysat for in seventh grade. They lived five houses from mine. I'm not sure how I knew they were Jewish. My parents had friends two houses away whose children went to a Catholic School and the neighbors across the street were Greek Orthodox. My best friend in elementary school went to a Unitarian Church. But other than them, I don't think I knew anyone's religion. In my neighborhood, religion was really not something that people talked about outside of their families.

About the time I was babysitting for the Jewish family, someone told me, but not my parents and I can't remember who, that Jews didn't believe in Jesus. That didn't strike me at that time as a particularly big deal since my only religious sentiment was the resentment I felt towards my Methodist grandmother's proselytizing. I wouldn't know until decades later that Jesus was Jewish.

I grew up in Middle America—middle class, Midwest, Michigan—brought up in a suburb of a college town. Our family went to my grandmother's downtown Free Methodist Church on Sundays. Going to church with my family structured the week, offering an opportunity to dress up and see a few relatives. My parents' friends and my school friends didn't attend that church. So it became obvious to me that religion played little or no role in the daily lives we led. One of my two brothers, the first child of course, continued

5

to attend another church on Sundays as an adult, and often with my parents.

The Methodists who adopted the word "free" in 1860 wanted to help the poor, wanted slaves to be freed and wanted pews to be free rather than rented or sold. Our Free Methodist Church, however, didn't project any of those values, values which I now find impressive. I certainly didn't learn about any of those freedoms in Sunday School. The younger of my two older brothers apparently didn't fully appreciate his freedom either because while we were sitting in Sunday services he would take out his jack knife and carve away the letters -THODIST that were printed on the pencils in the pews, leaving pencils for others that said FREE ME.

David

I DON'T RECALL FEELING more strongly about Israel or being Jewish when I returned to college, but after having spent nine months there I must have. What I remember best about my last two years of college was becoming serious about my studies. I had a great teacher, loved my classes, spent hours talking with friends about books and discovered there was little I enjoyed more than writing papers on Ancient Greek Philosophy. After I graduated, I entered a doctoral program and spent the next six years doing little more than reading, writing and playing basketball.

I completed my dissertation on Plato in 1980, and then moved to Brooklyn, and only there did Judaism enter my life as a serious possibility. It did so largely because I was spending a lot of time with my maternal grandfather. Ninety years old, he was almost totally blind and could barely hear, but he still lived alone in New London, Connecticut. My mother was worried about him, and she appreciated it when I would visit him for a weekend. I started doing it simply to please her, but it soon became something I valued for myself. A quiet, generous man with a dry wit who called himself a "Jewish Yankee" and was totally comfortable in his own skin, he was born on a Baron de Hirsch Farm in Chesterfield, a few miles outside of New London. A wealthy German Jew, de Hirsch funded immigration programs that brought poor eastern European Jews (like my great-grandfather) onto farms in the United States, Canada and Argentina.

As a young man, my grandfather moved into town and opened a hardware store, but he never lost his love of the soil. He kept a huge vegetable garden in the back of his New London house. Nor did he ever lose his deep connection to the Jewish community. In 1925 he and my grandmother helped found Congregation Beth El, and they often hosted the Kiddush at their home, which was just down the street. I remember being told as a young child in the 1950s that he was selling Israeli bonds to help support the new Jewish state in which he invested great hope. In 1980 he was living in an apartment a couple of blocks from the synagogue, to which he walked almost daily. I would arrive for my weekend visits on Friday, accompany him to Shabbat services and then to the Kiddush afterwards. The next morning we would return to the synagogue, usually to attend a Bar Mitzvah. My grandfather, well liked and widely admired in New London, knew everybody, old and young, and at Beth El he was totally at home.

My grandfather was neither a spiritual nor an educated man, and I imagine he would have had little to say if I had asked why he prayed every day or what he thought about God. His Judaism was mundane and its rhythms informed the only life he had ever known. He was a member of a community to which he gave much and by which he was sustained. Without it he would not have recognized himself.

Gina

My maternal grandmother wore her religion all day, singing hymns and judging me, particularly about what she thought was immodest clothing (a swimsuit), cursing (saying Geez), playing cards, and dancing. My parents suggested that she was simply a product of her time and deserved respect. They broke from church orthodoxy by choosing not to baptize their children. They thought we should make decisions about religion for ourselves as adults.

My maternal grandmother outlived my other grandparents and was the most vocally religious. She may have had a tough interior but she was overweight and rarely moved from her chair most of the day. When she was visiting she said grace before dinner, which was the only time when prayer was spoken in our house. She was generally quiet except when riled. My father could easily get a rise out of her by his invention of his "first wife." He would just say my first wife made better green beans, or did whatever better, and Grandma would growl a response. I remember her speaking of Revelations and suggesting that some apocalyptic event was about to happen any day.

My mother grew up in a small town in Michigan. Her parents' surnames were Hess, my grandmother, and Anderson, my grandfather, an accountant who died of Alzheimer's when I was eight. I assume, but without DNA testing, they were of German and Scandinavian ancestry. My father's parents' surnames, Crandell and Knickerbocker, suggest Irish and English origins. They were farmers in Michigan and also Methodists. In photos they appear thin and very serious. I remember that they gave us lemon drops when we visited them after church.

David

CHANTING IN UNISON WITH a congregation or drinking a glass of wine on Friday night had never appealed or meant a thing to me, but during those moments with my grandfather I came to admire, even to envy, the way he lived. It seemed so solid. I understood barely a word of Hebrew, but the tunes of the prayers are with me still.

Because I was his grandson, I was a somebody at Congregation Beth El and I had an inkling of what it would feel like to really be a part of such a place. But I wasn't, and when I returned to Brooklyn on Sundays, I returned to being a nobody. I was scraping by as a part-time instructor of philosophy at Baruch College. My college friends were now lawyers and doctors who were starting families and buying homes, while I was living alone, barely able to pay the rent.

One day I was glancing at the Classified Ads in the *New York Times* and happened upon a listing for a job as a math teacher at a private school. I needed the money and had always liked math, and so without giving it much thought decided to apply. My Ph.D., even though it was in Philosophy, must have impressed them, for I got the job. The school turned out to be Ramaz, a modern Orthodox Yeshiva on the Upper East side of Manhattan, which offered both a traditional religious and a contemporary secular education. Most of its students were worldly and academically ambitious, but also seriously engaged with their religion. Its faculty was composed of rabbis and laypeople, some of whom were like me: Jewish but not observant. I was, nonetheless, required to wear a yarmulke in school every day.

There was much I appreciated about Ramaz. The students were good natured, hard working and respectful, and I don't remember disliking one of them. A couple were more talented in math than me, but they weren't obnoxious about it. I hit it off with other teachers as well. One had his Ph.D. in history and we became friends. He was a smart, funny guy and, even though he was as secular as me, he had become pals with several of the younger rabbis. I became part of this odd little group. We all liked baseball and on one memorable weekday evening a few of us went to Shea Stadium together to see the New York Mets play the San Francisco Giants. On our way to the game we stopped at a kosher restaurant on the Lower East Side.

These young rabbis, I later heard, would not be working at Ramaz for long, since they planned to move to new settlements being built on the West Bank. I did not know a thing about the illegality of those settlements or who was displaced to make room for them. Nor did I wonder.

Gina

I HAVEN'T STUDIED CHRISTIANITY or Judaism or any other religions, nor read the Bible as a literary text. My memories of being a child in Sunday school do not include lessons about Christian values, such as mercy. Instead, I remember the Sunday school teachers, much like my grandmother, telling me what I should not do. (I learned a bit about mercy recently at the Museum of the Igreja da Misericórdia, a 17th-century church in Porto, Portugal, which presented a brief history of hospitals and medical tools, which were created as a Christian response to the misery of the poor.)

I wish I could remember when I first heard the word "antisemitism." Possibly it was when I learned about the Holocaust, maybe in a high school history course. Questions about the Holocaust plagued all the decades that followed: How could something of such violent magnitude have happened without protest? What did Germans and Americans know about Hitler's genocide at the time?

In high school I wasn't aware that anyone was Jewish. Looking back, I'm guessing that my French teacher, Mrs. Goldstein, was Jewish. I only found out years after I graduated that there were some Jewish students in my high school. One, Susan Jacoby, an accomplished author of more than a dozen books, didn't know she was Jewish either. She describes herself online as a secularist and an atheist. She was brought up Catholic and didn't know until she was 24 that her father was Jewish, which led her to write a book called *Half-Jew: A Daughter's Search for her Family's Buried Past.*

David

TWO MEMORIES OF MY brief stint at Ramaz are particularly vivid. On a warm afternoon in the Spring, I accompanied a group of boys to Central Park for a softball game. When we reached the field we had reserved, other, older guys were already there. I got into a heated argument with one of them and suddenly I became somebody I had never met before: a leader of a ragtag gang of yarmulke-wearing Yeshiva *bochers* who needed my protection from a raging antisemite (which the guy almost certainly wasn't). I lost my temper, and I think I called him an "asshole," but that's all I can remember. Did we play the game or not? Was my yelling coherent? Was I ashamed of the role which I had played with such unexpected vehemence? Or did it feel good to now be part of a long line of warriors that stretched from the Warsaw Ghetto to the Sinai Desert?

Second, I was one of several teachers who took a group of students to see a film. I'm pretty sure it was the 1982 documentary about the Holocaust, *Genocide*. I left the theater stunned. Of course I already knew about the Holocaust, but the images on the screen hit me with particular force, probably because I was there with the Ramaz students. Although all four of my grandparents had lived safely in the United States since well before Hitler's rise, and I knew of only one great-uncle who had been murdered in Europe, the yarmulke on my head felt like a yellow star identifying me as a potential victim. It was as if a wound I did not know I had received was suddenly opened.

Most memorable about that afternoon was a brief conversation I had with a girl who was in one of my math classes. Like many of the students at Ramaz, she was poised, stylishly dressed and indistinguishable from other wealthy teenagers on the Upper East Side. We were walking back to the school and, for what reason I cannot recall, I said to her, "I have never felt so Jewish in my life." To my amazement, she snapped at me. "What do you mean by that?" For her being Jewish was knowing Hebrew, reciting the prayers, going to synagogue, lighting candles, eating dinner with her family on shabbat, studying Talmud. Simply assuming the mantle of victimhood and claiming membership in the tribe was, by her lights, too easy.

Gina

GOING TO COLLEGE IN 1967 meant that opposing the war in Vietnam was the center of my politics, such as they were. Israel did not register in my thoughts even though the 1967 war was a landmark in Israel-Palestine history. In 1968, the Students for a Democratic Society chapter at Michigan State was very active, the second largest chapter (the internet now tells me) after Harvard at the time, in both opposing the war and supporting civil rights. I remember attending a meeting of SDS but the speakers were too aggressive for me to feel a part of the movement. Eventually, SDS turned violent and broke store windows at Jacobson's department store on Grand Avenue across from campus. After May 4, 1970, when four Kent State students protesting the war were shot and killed by Ohio National Guardsmen, classes were suspended. The Guardsmen were acquitted. That summer I traveled for seven weeks through eleven countries in Europe with a Eurorail Pass and *Europe on $5 a Day*.

In my twenties my break with religion was clarified. By then I had come to think that religion had imposed a subordinate role on women. I remember my enthusiasm when the first issue of *Ms Magazine*, founded by Gloria Steinem and Dorothy Pitman Hughes, came out in December, 1971. *Ms* seemed to me to spark a desperately needed conversation about women's rights in America. I felt great solidarity with women for it was a time of focusing on our bodies and how greatly our reproductive capacity had shaped our lives. I remember being invited to a women's gathering to investigate our bodies with speculums. I'm sure I would remember if I had attended. I became very attentive to language, admiring "women," thinking of "ladies" and "chicks" as cartoons. I remember developing a personal principle that I would continue to follow: women would receive respect prima facie; men would have to earn it.

Golda Meir's term as Prime Minister of Israel from 1969 to 1974 coincided with this but I knew nothing about her policies. I admired her simply because of the rarity of a female prime minister at that time. I admired Norway's first female Prime Minister, Gro Brundtland, for standing on the side of Labor and Environment but it was Prime Minister Margaret Thatcher who proved to me that women's policies could also be not that different than men's.

David

DURING MY TWO YEARS in New York from 1980 to 1982 my relationship with my grandfather and Congregation Beth El in New London deepened and I enjoyed teaching math at Ramaz. I was getting a sense of what being at home in a Jewish world might feel like. And it was compelling. As a result, when I received an offer of a tenure-track professorship at Iowa State University, I was tempted to turn it down. I did not want to abandon my life in New York, which felt filled with promise. Finally, however, the invitation to work in the field in which I was trained, and which I loved, was too good to pass up.

Full disclosure: when I was deliberating whether to move to Iowa or not, two other factors helped tip the scale. First, the woman with whom I had been involved broke up with me. Second, I had suffered a knee injury that required surgery, but I had no health insurance. I took the Iowa State job, but I sublet my Brooklyn apartment thinking I would return in a year with both my heart and my knee mended. But I never did.

Gina

IN MY MID-TWENTIES, AFTER teaching third grade near Kalamazoo for three years, I moved to Raleigh to earn a master's degree in landscape architecture at North Carolina State. I returned to Michigan to practice in an office until 1979 when I moved to Ames to teach landscape architecture at Iowa State University. Two years later I met David, who moved to Ames to teach philosophy, and we were married in 1984. A Plato scholar, he joked about being pagan but I knew his Jewish identity was, and remains, very deep. I'm not sure I could have identified what it was about him that was Jewish at that time. He told me he looked like a rabbi but I wouldn't have been able to recognize a stereotype like that.

He had lots of good energy. I wouldn't realize until decades later that his bursting energy was, in part, driven by hyperactivity, something that benefited me since he was always eager to make plans. We seemed similar in so many ways. Having the same work meant that we had a lot to talk about: our students, our colleagues, our critical view of the way things were. We liked biking, swimming and going to the beach (missing in Iowa). David knew so much more than me about music but I was game for going to concerts. I knew more about art but he was always willing to go to museums and to explore environmental art and landscape projects whether in Iowa, New York City or Europe.

In the summer a year after we were married, I got a grant to go to Italy to study sixteenth-century gardens. David said he didn't really like to travel. Over the years I would learn that he was a person of routines who quickly formed habits and traveling interfered with the daily structure he found so reassuring. But to my relief he wanted to go to Italy and learn Italian. We spent most of six weeks in Florence with trips to Rome, Venice, and Sicily. David took an Italian class in Florence while I figured out how to travel to some urban and some very remote gardens. Some days we walked for six hours. In Sicily we took a local bus from place to place. On our way to see the Greek temples at Agrigento, we had an argument about something I don't recall. Traveling requires much negotiation. What I remember is that this argument reached well beyond the volume and intensity that we were used to. I am easily embarrassed by drawing attention to myself and we were practically yelling. When I looked around to see who might be listening, I realized that others on the bus were talking loudly too and couldn't have cared less about what we were saying. I'm not sure this threw open my sense of reserve but it did feel good to be able to openly disagree.

David

AT FIRST I THOUGHT the boys were wearing yarmulkes. They
weren't. Instead, the many hats I saw on young male heads on
the Iowa State campus were caps with logos, not of teams, but of
Dekalb Seed or John Deere. It took me a while to adjust. But I did,
and it wasn't hard, for I quickly came to like Ames, Iowa. It was a
peaceful, sensible college town, filled with intelligent people, and
the fact that it was in what I took to be the middle of nowhere didn't
trouble me. After all, I was teaching Greek Philosophy and for the
first time in my life I had my own office. My colleagues in the Philosophy Department were first-rate and friendly. I could afford to
rent a large apartment and buy the car I had never needed in New
York. What was most foreign to me were the students. They were
quiet. I had grown up with an implicit assumption: smart people
talk a lot. During my first semester teaching at Iowa State I learned
this is not always the case. There was a young woman in one of
my classes who sat in the back row and never said a word. I was
stunned when I read her mid-term paper, which was on an early
Greek philosopher named Anaximander. It was extremely smart.

While I certainly would have preferred students who asked
more questions and came to my office to talk about books, being a
professor at Iowa State wasn't a bad job at all.

Two months after I arrived in Ames, and a couple of weeks
after my knee surgery, my colleague Joe and his wife Fern, both
of whom happened to be Jews from New York, invited me to a
Halloween party. That's where I met Gina, a professor of landscape
architecture. For a costume she had drawn cat whiskers on her
face. I was dressed as an uptight professor.

Our first date was at the one good restaurant in town, where
we had, and we talked about, scallops. Our second was dinner at
her place where we had a long conversation about living in Iowa.
Gina, who was born and raised in Michigan and did her graduate
work in North Carolina, had arrived three years earlier. Although
we both liked our jobs and the town, our responses to being far

from home were different. Mine was infused with a sense of loss. Yes, I was a professor and a member of an academic community, but my roots in Ames were shallow compared to what my grandfather had in New London and the Ramaz kids had in New York. Having tasted a life organized around traditions, rituals, texts and a synagogue, I was now on my own and I felt much had been lost. By contrast, for Gina, being in Ames meant possibility. She was the only one in her family who had graduated from a university and then left Michigan. Charting her own course, being free from the expectations that came with being a woman born in 1949 was energizing for her. She didn't miss traditions one bit or suffer the least bit of nostalgia. To my credit, I found our differences to be invigorating.

Two years later, in April of 1984, we got married in a courthouse in Nevada, Iowa, on a weekday afternoon. Our only guests were two friends who served as witnesses. We stopped on our way back home to open a bottle of champagne in a cornfield. As our matchmaker Fern confessed a few years later, she didn't think we would last. I can see why.

Gina is reserved. For her language is a tool that should be deployed only when it is truly needed to get something done. Silence is her default, especially when she's thinking hard or angry. For me, language, out loud, in my head and on the page, is the lifeblood of reality, and I can't make sense of things without it.

A worrier and a planner, restless and always a step ahead of myself, I often miss what's standing before my eyes. Gina inhabits the present more than anyone I have ever known, and as a result she often loses track of time. I never do. I am punctual to a fault and never miss a deadline.

Gina is a practical thinker. Whether it's in her work as a landscape architect or anywhere else, she's great at tackling a problem that can be solved. She takes it a step at a time, proceeds carefully and is incredibly patient. Mine is a jumpy intellect that is easily distracted. I revel in questions and overviews, and delight in discovering absurdities. At my best, I can be serious, smart and funny all at the same time. At my worst, I'm facile.

I do most things too fast. I wolf down my dinner and sometimes when it's gone I realize I paid no attention to its taste. It takes me seconds to decide what to order in a restaurant and minutes to buy clothes or shoes. Too often I find myself skimming rather than reading, and I miss more than I'd care to admit. I used to love basketball, with its constant running and rapid-fire turns, but I never really took to the slow pace of baseball. I can't linger in front of a painting in a museum. Gina is almost never in a rush. She savors delicious food, spends hours, sometimes days, making decisions about what to buy, and loves to look at landscapes and art.

Gina feels absolutely no attraction to anything religious, which she thinks is by and large didactic and oppressive. Although it's never occurred to me to take seriously the possibility that the world was created by a loving God, I find people who believe this to be interesting. William James' book, *Varieties of Religious Experience*, expresses my views better than I ever could. James holds that, whether or not God actually exists, the impulse that animates believers is an essential feature of human consciousness. Simply to dismiss religion as ridiculous or nonsensical is thus a fundamental mistake.

Gina

ALTHOUGH I HAD JEWISH friends in Ames before we were married, soon I had many more. As the years passed, I gradually began to feel a little bit like an insider. I recognized a few Yiddish words. I could say the word "Jew" without feeling like an antisemite. I went to my first seders. Soon I became familiar with our Jewish friends' geographic references, especially New York City. Jewishness seemed to radiate from there. David once told me that he didn't like being asked if he was from New York for it seemed an indirect way of asking if he was Jewish.

I also became adept at recognizing potentially Jewish names. At first, the questions were asked of me: Did I know that a friend was Jewish? Did I know that so-and-so or a notable person was Jewish? Did I know Paul Newman was Jewish? (Actually only his father was.) One of my students at Iowa State asked me how I could not know that he was Jewish since his name was Levy. But I was not in the habit of asking these kinds of questions, or placing such emphasis on ethnicity or where people were from. No other student expected me to know that their name was Norwegian or that they were Lutheran. Although identifying Jewish names was initially new to me, progressively it became an inner routine of my own. I would ask myself: Was the person I was just being introduced to or reading about Jewish? Is the financier Jewish just because his name sounds like he might be?

This practice is something that now feels annoying to me, like a nagging addiction. I don't fully understand why I ask myself these questions. Why does it matter? What would it tell me about a stranger I have just met? Or someone I've only heard about? Apart from their names, is there something else about them that makes them seem Jewish? But now that I have internalized this question, unfortunately I find it hard to stop.

I was mystified by why most of our Jewish friends in Ames, many of whom were not married to Jews and none of whom were members of a synagogue, were so tied to calling themselves Jewish.

Just as I had always thought that being Christian meant membership in a Church, I assumed that being Jewish meant membership in a Congregation. For me, being religious required actively practicing a faith in a community that shaped daily life. I had easily abandoned the self-description of "Christian" because I was secular. But most of the Jews I knew, and know today, would describe themselves as secular Jews. This seemed strange to me. David always corrects me if, for example, I say Chinese or Korean instead of Chinese American or Korean American when I'm talking about someone in the U.S. But I've never heard him describe a Jew as Jewish American. What is the difference?

While our Jewish friends, like most Americans, were cognizant of the Holocaust and the history of antisemitism, none had actually suffered from ethnic or religious discrimination themselves. David certainly hadn't. They read the same books, ate the same kinds of food, enjoyed the same movies and music, had the same goals for their children and were liberal Democrats just like us. Increasingly I wondered what it was exactly that our friends were clinging to when they didn't know a word of Hebrew and had little interest in what actually goes on in a synagogue. What did it mean for people who were so much like me, someone who chose not to practice religion, to identify as Jews? What did it mean for David?

One thing it did mean, at least for him, was being left wing. David's parents were very active in civil rights groups, as were many of their Jewish friends. These were qualities I admired, though David was dismissive of what their Peace group meetings could actually accomplish. Nevertheless, for many years, I've heard him talk, usually with much pride, about his left-wing credentials. He loves to tell people he was a *real* red-diaper baby. His father, who had been accused of being a communist and then was fired from his job as an engineer for New York City, had wheeled him around in a stroller in Central Park at a demonstration supporting the Stockholm peace petition in 1951. David has mentioned the Rosenberg trials many times and also takes pride in growing up on a street in New Jersey where almost all of his neighbors were

Black. Yet, I wondered, wasn't it his parents who were pushing the stroller and decided to move into an integrated neighborhood, and not him?

Did his parents' activism have anything to do with being Jewish? Italians, Catholics, Irish folks, many people were activists. Was David suggesting through the example of his parents that Jews are more attuned to injustice? Was it because they had suffered it? That may well be the case for the generation of his parents who were adults during WWII, as well as those who were college students in the early 60s.

In 1964, thousands of African Americans in Mississippi who organized Freedom Summer through their church networks to register Black voters were joined by more than a thousand out-of-state volunteers, many of whom were Jewish. I remember the terrible news of that summer when three Jewish and African American men were murdered by the Ku Klux Klan. Clearly, many young Jews had translated their understanding of the Holocaust into civil rights activism. But what about the next generation, like David's, whose childhoods were not an experience of injustice but of upward mobility? Was our generation, was David, simply adopting the left-wing mantle, nearly bragging about it, from college in the 70s followed by a comfortable job in the 80s?

He is so proud of his left-wing heritage, though he's no longer politically active, that he still repeats stories about his participation in the protests against the Vietnam War. But that War was more than fifty years ago. Is clinging to a left-wing identity that is now an abstraction like clinging to his Jewish identity?

I didn't usually know the religious background of our non-Jewish friends in Iowa, but there were a few exceptions. One close friend who had actually grown up in Iowa, told us that as a child she attended a very open-minded Swedish Lutheran church, which she enjoyed. The reason she told us about it was to explain how puzzled she was that her brother had turned to the far right of the Lutheran Church and American politics. A colleague of mine, with whom I had a cordial working relationship and whose daughter had playdates with mine, was an evangelical Christian. We talked about the vernacular and modern landscape but not religion. David had a colleague in the Religion Department who had been a Methodist minister, a peace and civil rights organizer, and a member of Ames Friends Meeting. He organized a Quaker-style funeral that made a lasting impression on me. Everyone was sitting around in an ordinary room at the University, without leadership, and largely in silence, until someone, anyone, in the group felt the urge to speak. The silences were as profound as the words.

David

THAT GINA HAD BEEN raised as a (nominal) Methodist did not cause me a moment of hesitation nor did it bother my parents at all. In fact, the only question any of our four parents ever asked us was whether our getting married was okay with the other's parents. But I was never sure what it meant to my grandfather. Of his six grandchildren, only one married a Jew. I assume he was disappointed, but he never complained or criticized any of us. Still, it made me a little sad that we did not have a real wedding in which he would have recited a blessing in Hebrew. I wouldn't have understood the words but I'd probably have recognized the tune.

We got married in April and later that Spring we threw a party for our friends in Ames and in the summer both our parents threw parties for us. One was in Michigan, the other in Southbury, Connecticut, where my parents had retired, mainly because my mother wanted to live near her father. Both were large, welcoming and pleasant. Our parents themselves, however, did not meet until we moved to Brookline, Massachusetts, more than a decade later. Gina's folks were visiting us from Michigan and the six of us went to a restaurant on a highway, halfway between Brookline and Southbury. I remember it being cordial and not the least bit awkward, but I don't think our parents ever saw each other again.

We hit some rough patches during those first years of marriage. A bad one came during the summer of 1985. Gina had received a grant to do research on Italian Renaissance gardens, and I tagged along. We travelled throughout the country, from Sicily to Venice. One evening we were in Bologna. I was hungry and wanted to pop into the first restaurant we saw that wasn't crowded. Gina wanted to find something better and she was willing to take the time to do it. Unfortunately, I prevailed. The food was mediocre, she was sullen, I felt guilty. As usual, my impulse was to get over it by talking, but she refused. For her what was done was done, no amount of talking could change that, and this drove me crazy.

I don't think her silent treatment or our unhappiness lasted too long, though, for most of my memories of that trip are very good.

Back in Ames, some of our worst fights came after ordinary social events, especially those that involved Fern and Joe. They were both big talkers from New York, and I felt completely at ease in their company. Gina, though, would often clam up and barely say a word. When we got home, I would comment on what a nice time we'd just had, and then she would say something about Joe being a bully and a phoney. Because he'd been a good, supportive colleague to me, and had become a trusted friend, I'd come to his defense, and we'd go at it. Gina would sometimes burst into tears, of anger not grief, and then clam up again, which made me crazy. I wanted to talk more, she less.

Gradually, we learned to live with each other. We landed on solid ground when our first daughter was born in 1986. We both delighted in our child and, even during her first three months when she cried every night for a few hours before going to sleep, we were glad to share the work of taking care of her. Our second daughter arrived in 1989. With identical jobs and salaries, and two energetic children, we split parenting pretty equally. Since we were both writing books, and we each needed to devote one day on the weekend to work, I went to my office on Saturdays while she stayed home with the girls, and on Sundays I would take them out somewhere while she was working at home. On weekdays we brought the girls to Linda, a former pediatric nurse who lived on a farm a few miles outside of town. After her kids entered school, she took care of our two children and four others whose parents were friends of ours. They loved it there.

There's a saying of Confucius I've liked for a long time. "At fifteen I set my heart upon learning. At thirty I planted my feet firm upon the ground." That seems to do a good job of describing my own timeline. Except for a love of sports and a desire to emulate my parents in their political activism, I was adrift and clueless until I got to college and discovered I wanted to study philosophy. But then it took me another decade before I had a full, stable, nourishing life to go along with it. I planted my feet upon the ground in

Ames, Iowa, and I hope never to feel anything but gratitude for my thirteen years there.

Gina

RIDING IN THE CAR with David, the year I precisely remember as 1986, he described our future children as "half-breeds." It didn't seem to be a joke. I fell into tears. I was seven months pregnant. David was certainly not comparing humans to dogs. But was he suggesting that the difference in our parents' religions was equivalent to us being separate breeds? Was it some sort of weird atavism that led him to make this comment? Did he think Jews were a separate race? What kind of thinking led him to use this ugly phrase, which had once been contemptuously applied to the offspring of an American Indian and a European person? I had to conclude that it was a throwback to some kind of tribalism that David no longer took seriously. I simply decided to let it go and move forward.

Before our children were born, it was important to me not to give up my name since doing so would be a throwback to a time when women were owned by their husbands. So we decided that, if they were girls, they would have my last name, a bit of a matrilineal line, and if they were boys, David's. He agreed on the condition that he got to pick the first names, which is a Jewish tradition. Fortunately, we especially liked both of David's grandmothers' names and they became our daughters' first names. The only time I recall our different surnames being a problem was when David was referred to as Mr. Crandell in the hospital. In fact, I thought that our decision about names was such a good one that everyone would be doing it before the girls were grown. But we have only known two other families who ever did.

Since we were tied to neither, we celebrated both Hanukkah and Christmas. For Hanukkah we all sang the Jewish prayer over the candles, the only time in our house that we prayed, if you can count chanting a few Hebrew words that we couldn't translate as praying. I think I enjoyed the candles more than anyone else in the family. I loved watching the flames after David and the girls had wandered away, until the last one expired and the trail of smoke rose above it. Later I found that the family stayed around longer if we made bets on which candle would go out last. In recent years, especially if our daughters are not at home, we often invite friends to share candles with us.

David said from the beginning that he did not want a Christmas tree. This was fine with me since I thought the whole Santa and shopping thing was out of control. But I had a collection of ornaments that were meaningful to me so I started draping a garland across the mantle of the fireplace to which we added lights, ornaments, and some gifts below. It's a tradition to this day.

At Iowa State I had an Israeli colleague, the first Israeli I knew, who lived just a few houses from us. She was poised and very sure of herself, often saying "of course" as if to suggest that no matter what you told her she already knew it. She made donuts for the children on Hanukkah. We worked together on several projects and she made beautiful drawings. We were quite close but I don't remember us talking much about Israel. I knew she was from Tel Aviv and she made a point of saying that Israel was a tiny country, maybe only a third the size of Iowa, which seemed to suggest its inherent vulnerability. I assumed she didn't include the occupied territories. In fact, Israel is only one-seventh the size of Iowa.

In a conversation the subject of which I can't recall, I vividly remember her saying, "Arabs," and then, to my surprise, shaking her head as if to indicate her utter distaste, followed by a wave of her hand as if to brush them away. It was upsetting that she would speak this way about a whole group of people, millions in fact, but I didn't know enough to ask the questions I should have. Why did she think that? Did she actually know any Arabs? What had Arabs done to make her say that?

As I think back to those days in Ames I ask myself whether I had known any Arabs or Muslims. I thought the answer was no. But now I realize that I had both Arab and Muslim colleagues. I hadn't realized this before because, like me, they were people who said little about their ethnicity or religion. One invited me and other colleagues to his home for Turkish coffee several times. I didn't know what country he was from until I googled him recently and found out that he was born in Syria. I assume he was Muslim, but I don't know for sure. I do remember, however, that he recommended a book by Edward Said to me. Unfortunately I didn't follow up on it at that time. Mostly we talked about our shared interests in community and regional planning.

Two colleagues, who were married, were architects. She was from a prominent family in Istanbul. We socialized together many times. Once when they were at our home for dinner, David asked her if she was Muslim and she said yes. Her husband was from Princeton, NJ, and I think his father was a Christian minister. They moved to Istanbul a few years later.

I also had a fair number of Malaysian students who came to Iowa to study. (I once heard that it was because they thought that Iowa was the center of the U.S., which could only be concluded by looking at a very small map of the whole country. Whatever the reason, after the first students came, word-of-mouth brought many more.) They were Muslims and I now have doubts about my decision then not to let them leave class to pray.

David arranged for our young children to go to Sunday school in a space that a church shared with the Ames Jewish congregation. He said it was because there were so few Jews in Iowa and he wanted our daughters to have a sense of being Jewish. He also acknowledged that it would give us the time to enjoy reading the Sunday *New York Times*. I didn't ask myself many questions at the time about how our daughters might identify as Jewish. I only recall being at services once. And being quite surprised by the size of the donation David gave to a congregation with which we had so little interaction. It was much more than we have given to any organization in our lives before this past year. What was that about?

Once I overheard our daughter tell a friend, while they were collaborating on a drawing with crayons, that Daddy was Jewish and Mommy was Christian. I was shocked. But her six-year-old friend was not. She replied with the confidence of someone who had already debated religious issues: "I don't even believe in God." Later it made sense to me why our daughter identified me as

Christian. While their father spoke often of being Jewish, I certainly never said I was Christian. But for many years we visited my parents in Florida for our winter vacation. My parents did not go to church when we were there but they had a Christmas tree and we opened presents together.

Since I couldn't imagine calling myself Christian I felt the need to explain this to our daughters. In trying to correct their misconception I learned something about myself. I told my daughters that their father was Jewish and their mother was a feminist. I realized that it was women who had become my ethnicity, my community, and my closest source of cultural identity.

David

THE WINTERS IN IOWA were unimaginably cold and the summers brutally hot, and there were no mountains, lakes or forests nearby, but we liked it there. We both got tenure at Iowa State, had decent salaries, housing was affordable. Raising children was made easier by the flexibility our jobs afforded us and how small the town was. Best of all, we had good friends, all of whom were professors and also had young children. All but one of our group were transplants whose only reason for coming to Iowa was for a job. Had any of us been able to choose a place to live, it certainly wouldn't have been on the vast flatness of the American Midwest. The best Ames could offer as a cultural diversion was the occasional Town & Gown Chamber Music concert. The great lesson we learned there was that if we wanted to have some fun, we had to make it for ourselves. We often shared dinners with friends. Good company, good food, plenty to drink, lots of kids.

I remember one ridiculously cold Saturday morning in February. Gina and I were sitting over coffee, feeling gloomy at being housebound, and on the spot we decided to have a party that night. We started making calls, and despite the short notice everyone we invited came. No one had anything else to do. We got drunk, danced and laughed with people we liked. It was sort of wonderful, really.

Such, I think, is the deep paradox of community. It may be a rich and wonderful feature of human life, but it is generated by a negative: the need we have for one another to make up for what we lack. It often seems that the greater that need is, the stronger the community will be. Who knows, maybe it's the persecution they faced for so many centuries in Europe that has fueled the extraordinary sense of identification Jews feel with their tribe. Even I, as assimilated as they come, was susceptible to this impulse. I wanted us to join the one and only Jewish congregation in Ames. It was tiny and its nickname was "the little *schul* on the prairie." A rabbi-in-training from Hebrew Union College in Cincinnati visited once a month and during the high holidays. Gina had no objections and she was one of several non-Jewish spouses who were welcomed there.

Although my Jewishness never made me feel separate or in any way vulnerable in Ames, I was glad to be part of a Jewish community and help support it with my membership dues. Rarely, though, did I ever attend services there. A kind of fake nostalgia for a past that never really was? A need to belong even if I didn't? An homage, or apology, to my grandfather? The germination, however minimal, of a seed planted during my months on Kfar HaNassi?

Gina

I BELONGED TO A small group of women artists and writers, mostly professors, that met religiously, late afternoons on Fridays, in one of our homes to celebrate the end of the work week with a glass of beer or wine. Sometimes there were only a few of us, other times many more, depending on the season and the host. The group had been meeting for many years before I came, and continued for decades after I left. I was dedicated to this core community of women and it is what I have missed most about leaving Iowa.

Another of David's colleagues in the Religion Department, whose father was a German immigrant and Methodist minister, conceived of Jesus to be a defender of the oppressed. His wife, Esther, occasionally attended the Friday Club, as we called our women's group, and I will never forget what she once said. She had come to think Holocaust accounts had become "tiresome." I was aghast. I couldn't believe anyone could think that about the enormous suffering Jews had experienced. Even if she felt she had heard too much about the Holocaust I was shocked she would say it. I told David when I got home but he calmly responded with his familiar humor, the kind that flips expectations upside down: It's true. Jews can be tiresome.

One of the core members of the Friday Club was a good friend who had actually introduced David and me. I would describe her as an enthusiastic Jew. Fern, and her husband Joe, grew up on Long Island. They were, as David described them, big talkers that he felt totally at ease with. But I did not. I never had this problem with Friday Club or faculty meetings but with them I recall entire evenings where they talked so much I didn't say a word. Toward the end of one evening, sensing my silence I remember they said something like, tell us about landscape architecture. I'm also not one to be told what to talk about so that question didn't lead toward much conversation. David suggested I plan ahead of time what to say. This was a life lesson. Who knew? I think of conversation as something that begins spontaneously and moves undirected. But big talkers change that dynamic.

David's advice has become very useful over the years. Professors can be very repetitive and will, if given the chance, speak for 50 minutes. This explains big talkers. They practice a lot. I would call this repetition rather than conversation but performance depends upon repetition and is a weakness of mine. Maybe conversation, as I think of it, is really best between two people, although when there aren't too many big talkers, a small group can have what I would call a really good conversation. When I'm in a social situation I've learned to jump into the conversation early and repeat a story I've told before (they do get better with practice, if also more fictional) to avoid being trapped listening to someone who is overbearing.

Fern's vocabulary was sprinkled with Yiddish words. From her I learned that many Yiddish words sound more like what they mean than their English counterparts. She was annoyed by the number of people who said Merry Christmas so she made it clear that we should instead say the generic Happy Holidays. She was always on the lookout for comments that might be antisemitic. She avidly supported civil rights and the right to abortion.

She was a writer who spoke frequently about Jewish authors and wrote for a Jewish audience who she said were the largest group of book buyers. Her marriage lasted until just before their 20th anniversary when she found out her husband was having a relationship with one of his students. We were all shocked. Unlike many people who would bury this and stay with him, or bury this and leave him, in her anger she went straight to her computer to turn what he'd done into creative nonfiction. She didn't hesitate to tell the Friday Club or anyone else in our little college town who wanted to know. I truly admired the honesty it took for her to be so outspoken. But no one from my Midwestern milieu would have been so revengeful or so public. They divorced. Now she's married to a man who grew up in a Lebanese-American Catholic family in Ohio.

David

DURING THE 1980's I became a subscriber to *The New Republic*, whose owner then was Martin Peretz, a staunch Zionist. I remember being surprised how fiercely this famously liberal magazine defended American military support for Israel. Only a decade earlier, the war in Vietnam had ended in catastrophe and many Americans had not recovered from the tragedy of our country's misguided militarism. Precisely because it was unexpected, I found *The New Republic*'s hawkishness to be provocative, and close to attractive. I suspect that had you asked me to boil down my position in those days I would have said that, given the history of European anti-semitism, Jews needed and deserved Israel as their homeland. Surrounded by enemies, they had to protect themselves, and America should help them do so. Had you asked me about the people who lived there before European Jews began to arrive, I probably would have said that Palestine was an under-populated backwater of the Ottoman Empire whose land was owned by absentee landlords and had been neglected for centuries. Like Jason and Ruth in Kfar HaNassi, the Zionists had brought the place back to life by planting trees, draining the swamps and making the desert bloom. Despite knowing next to nothing about Palestinians and what they had suffered in 1948, I probably believed they were filled with hate and obstructed every good faith Israeli attempt to make peace.

Gina

PROTESTS FLARED ON CAMPUSES across the country in the late 80s supporting the overthrow of apartheid, which had existed in South Africa from 1948 to 1992. I remember the student protests at Iowa State to which President Robert Parks responded by saying that steps were underway to immediately divest the University of its stock in companies doing business in South Africa. (That's quite a contrast to today's hedge-fund universities that call the police to arrest students who ask them to divest from Israel.) Nelson Mandela was released from prison in 1990 and I knew the negotiations between the ANC and the government went on for several years. Of course I supported Black South Africans but not because I knew the details of their history. I typically supported the one who seemed to be the underdog. But this cause felt far away and remote from the U.S. and I wasn't actively involved.

I attended a lecture by Edward Said in Ames in 1991, which David was unable to attend. I remember feeling like I was taking his place. So, untypically for me, I sat in the center aisle near the front. When it was time for questions, though I am usually too shy, I asked Dr. Said the first question, one I thought David would have asked: Why hadn't Arab countries aided Palestinians? I wish I could remember what David had said that led me to that question. I don't think I really knew what I was asking. Only looking back can I begin to ask questions. Was it a particular historical event where Arab armies had failed? Were all Arabs thought similar enough to one another to always be allies? Or was it just a way to transfer the blame away from Israel to Arab countries?

Since that lecture, I've developed a deep respect for Said, an American academic born in a Palestinian Christian family in Jerusalem in 1935. In January, 1999, he wrote an Op-Ed, "The One-State Solution," for the *New York Times* following the collapse of the Netanyahu government after the failure of the Oslo II Accord to create two States. Said recognized that the failure of Israeli-Palestinian peace processes was that they had never acknowledged the inherent Zionist rejection of equality for Palestinians going back to 1948. Only a binational state with equal rights would bring peace. Said concluded with a generous and compassionate understanding of the history Palestinians shared with Israelis as victims and refugees: "Oslo required us to forget and renounce our history of loss, dispossessed by the very people who taught everyone the importance of not forgetting the past. Thus we are the victims of the victims, the refugees of the refugees."

David

DURING OUR YEARS IN Ames I don't remember thinking or talking much about Israel or the Palestinians, although it's possible that I did deliver the occasional lecture on this subject to Gina. My primary concerns during my thirteen years there were with what has turned out to be my life's work—trying to show how Ancient Greek Philosophy offers a desperately needed alternative to the modern technological worldview—raising my children, and enjoying the company of good friends.

Only two stories need recounting here. Our friend Fern told us that once she was approached by an older couple in the Ames Public Library. Apparently they knew she was Jewish. In a polite, straightforward and Iowan manner, they asked her if she could give them any tips on how to make money. Second, Gina and I were at some sort of departmental gathering, when Esther, the wife of one of my older colleagues, happened to say—apropos of what I have no idea—that she found Jews who talk about the Holocaust to be tiresome. I didn't find this remark offensive or threatening. Instead, I laughed and said something like, "Yeah, it's true. Jews can be tiresome."

I'm not sure why I reacted this way. Did I actually mean what I said? Had I begun to suspect that the persistent demand placed upon Americans to acknowledge Jewish victimhood might not always be entirely innocent? I doubt it. Perhaps Esther's remark did not sting because being Jewish had little to do with the good, comfortable life I was leading in Ames, Iowa. And, to be honest, she struck me as a foolish person, not worth taking seriously.

Gina

IN OUR FORTIES WE moved to Brookline when our daughters were six- and eight-years old. Rather than belonging to a singular State University Town, we now lived where there were dozens of universities within easy reach. Furthermore, from our house, in five minutes, we could walk to a Kosher grocery, Judaica Art and Israel Book stores if we wanted, as well as three synagogues. There was little need for our children to go to Sunday school to learn about Jewish culture here.

On her first day of summer camp, a week after we moved, our eight-year-old daughter asked us if we kept kosher. We were not in Iowa anymore. At the nearby playground the same week, our daughter met a new friend and came running to ask us: Which is farther away? Russia or Iowa? To my surprise at that time our bank had a sign posted that said—Russian spoken here—to accommodate an influx of Russian Jews to Brookline. Public schools were closed during the high holidays. In our neighborhood we saw Hasidic women wearing wigs and men wearing side curls with dark hats, pushing strollers. But the heads of our friends were secularly bare and many of their marriages as "mixed" as ours.

Very soon after we moved, new words began to appear in our daughters' vocabularies. In Brookline, they played "homeless," something they hadn't known about in Iowa. There they called their game "orphans." Both games were essentially playing house without parents in charge. While we were driving around Boston, they would point to places, under bridges and alongside parks, where they imagined they could make homes to sleep for the night. When "SATs" sneaked into their vocabulary we knew the word was from Brookline, a town where even elementary school kids talked about getting into the right college. Instead of one State university, there were Harvard, MIT, and fifty others around Boston. These new words said so much about moving to a city from a small town: the diversity was so much broader.

David

IOWA STATE HAD BEEN a good place for me to begin my career. My colleagues were supportive, unpretentious, intelligent and friendly. There was not an asshole among them, a fact, as I later learned, is hardly the norm in my business. My first Chair was a gentle, decent, thoughtful man. When I first arrived he sat me down and told me what I would need to do in order to get tenure: publish an article a year, do well in the classroom, be a good citizen of the department. Very straightforward; very Iowan. After I got my first couple of articles in print, the pressure was off, and my professional life was largely stress-free. As a professor at Iowa State I could concentrate on work I wanted to do without worrying about my status in the larger academic world. In retrospect, this was a marvelous luxury, especially compared to the relentless competition, self-promotion and anxiety that permeates the contemporary university. I am incredibly lucky to have begun my career prior to the advent of the Internet.

For me the great negative at Iowa State was that it was primarily dedicated to science and engineering. As a result, the Philosophy Department played a marginal role. While I met dozens of smart undergraduates there, most majored in technical fields and could afford to take only one or two electives during their four years of college. A tiny number majored in Philosophy and even fewer had any interest in Plato or Aristotle. And so, when I was offered a tenured position at Boston University, with thriving programs in Philosophy, Classics and the other disciplines in the humanities, and the chance to teach graduate students, I was mighty tempted. Still, I hesitated. I liked Ames, had good friends there and my children were flourishing. Most important, Gina was a Full Professor of Landscape Architecture, and I had no intention of asking her to give up her job for my benefit. It turned out, however, that she was more certain about our move than I. Never having lived in a city before, she was eager for something new. Unlike me, she had no fear of leaving the security that comes with being a tenured professor. She was confident she could figure out things for herself. And she did. For the past thirty years she has held a variety of positions at Harvard, Rhode Island School of Design, Berkeley, Ohio State, Northeastern and the Boston Architectural College. She has been an editor at a journal, volunteered for non-profits and become politically active. As far as I can tell, she has no regrets about our decision to leave Ames. Nor do I.

In October of 1995, four months after having moved to Brookline, a town with a large Jewish population that borders Boston, I attended Kol Nidre services at Kehillath Israel, a congregation three blocks from our new home. I'm not sure what I'd been expecting, but whatever it was I was disappointed. The synagogue was huge and packed with people dressed to the nines, most of whom did not seem particularly engaged by the liturgy. I recall a poised and polished rabbi making a plea for donations. The place reminded me far more of my suburban synagogue in New Jersey, which I despised, than it did of Beth El in New London, and it was worlds apart from the self-propelled little *schul* in Ames, Iowa. Everything about it left me cold and while walking home I knew I would never return.

Gina

DURING OUR FIRST FULL summer in Brookline, 1996, I taught two urban design classes in Boston for Iowa State landscape architecture students. This included visiting public spaces in the city, such as Frederick Law Olmsted's Emerald Necklace and many sites that formed the urban fabric. Among sites we explored was the Holocaust Memorial. It is a work of public art on the Freedom Trail, near the historic Faneuil Hall. When I told David that I had taken my students to the Holocaust Memorial, he had the prerogative, for whatever reasons, to ask a question about it that I would not have even been able to think: Why is there a Holocaust Memorial in Boston? I was stunned by his question. I knew his question was not criticism of the design of the Memorial. I knew he was not questioning the Holocaust. What was he really questioning about the Memorial? The Holocaust carried such enormous emotional weight that I could not have asked myself his question. Nor did I even understand fully what he meant by it at the time.

For several years after we moved, I was Senior Editor of *Land Forum: The International Review of Landscape Architecture, Garden Art, Environmental Planning and Urban Design,* and also worked on books for Spacemaker Press in Cambridge. We published more than a hundred books about landscape architecture, one of which I now recall was *Shlomo Aronson: Making Peace with the Land* (1999), the first monograph about an Israeli landscape architect. I asked my Israeli colleague at Iowa State to review the book. Aronson's practice was probably the largest in Israel at that time and included many urban projects, such as the sacred Old City in East Jerusalem, and many large parks. One I remember from photographs was the Dead Sea, where the design brought attention to the depth of the lowest park on Earth: Long horizontal walls that followed contours adjacent to roadways identified in blue tiles each hundred meters below sea level. Another was Beit Guvrin-Maresha National Park, an archeological park of 1250-acres, one of a number of them featured in the book. Why would Israel be so devoted to archaeology? (Little did I know at the time that the archeological project Aronson was working on was both an excavation and a cover-up.)

David

SOON AFTER WE ARRIVED, we decided to explore Boston by walking on the Freedom Trail, a 2.5-mile-long path that passes famous historic places such as the Old North Church and Bunker Hill. While we were doing so we stumbled upon the newly opened Holocaust Memorial. It is a striking work of architecture, whose six glass towers reference the six million Jews who were murdered. But it wasn't the design that hit me hard. It was a question: what in the world was it doing here, just across the street from the Union Oyster House, which bills itself as the oldest restaurant in the United States? As far as I knew, Jews hadn't played much of a role in the American Revolution or, in subsequent centuries, in this, the oldest part of Boston. Abruptly, with no contextualization whatsoever, the six towers arose and exhorted passersby to remember Jewish suffering. I found this unsettling. Certainly not because I think anyone should forget the Holocaust. No, the Memorial felt like a kind of bullying. The project, I later read, had been initiated by survivors of Nazi concentration camps who had settled in Boston. No doubt, they were honestly motivated to do what they could to prevent any resurgence of the horrors they themselves experienced. Still, I couldn't help but wonder what sort of political muscle had been flexed in order to place these six glass towers in the middle of colonial Boston. Gina, I think, was surprised I even raised this question. As the years passed, though, she began to think about it far more rigorously than I ever had.

Gina

OUR DAUGHTERS ATTENDED BROOKLINE High School and colleges in New York. The younger one spent her junior year of high school in Beijing. She returned, ironically, with the incentive to learn more about Western culture. Our older daughter attended the Birthright program in Israel during a summer in college because it was a free trip and her high school friends were going. Even though she was shocked by the constant presence of young soldiers her age carrying assault weapons, the family story, repeatedly told, is that when she came home she described Israel as "our land." (She now describes her Birthright experience as brainwashing.)

I've been asked by several people whether I brought up our children Jewish. Unless we regularly attended a synagogue the answer is obviously no. But I think the question was asking something else, which I don't understand. Our daughters, if asked today, would likely identify themselves, in part, as culturally Jewish. They appreciate their father's and grandparents' Jewish stories, have a fondness for Hanukkah, and may pay closer attention than most to what they see or hear about Jews. Though I don't think they seek out Jewish friends, one of our daughters has always had a few and the other has had many, some going back to elementary school. But since the War on Gaza began, and for some time before that, she has been unable to talk with her friends about Israel. I am not surprised by this. That discussion seems to be off the table for people we know as well. Our daughters' political views are similar to ours, though one leans more socialist and the other avoids political conflict. But the work they both do today, I am very proud to say, is fully engaged in helping people who face dire medical and housing crises, making it much more socially activist than anything either of their parents ever did.

David

THINGS WORKED OUT WELL for me at Boston University. Working with graduate students, teaching strong undergraduates and being part of what was, for a long while, a genuinely liberal arts university felt like a gift. I retired in 2020 for many reasons, not least of which was that BU had gradually morphed into a privatized version of the Iowa State University of Science and Technology. Its mission was no longer to educate but to become a highly ranked research institution whose graduates got high-paying jobs in finance and tech. Obsessed with its brand, it dutifully abided by the standard corporate imperative "get big or die." Still, I am immensely grateful to BU for giving me a chance to move beyond the narrow academic confines of Iowa State.

I am also grateful that we landed in Brookline. It's a good town that combines the best of two worlds: the urban and the suburban. On the suburban side, ours is a quiet, tree-lined street, there are excellent parks, libraries and public schools nearby, and our police, firefighters and sanitation services are reliable. On the urban side, we're close to Boston and Cambridge and all their cultural riches. Public transportation is decent and biking is relatively safe. For many years we did not own a car.

Not surprisingly, because of all its advantages, housing costs in Brookline have skyrocketed, but back in 1995 people like us could afford to live here.

Gina

MY MIDWESTERN AND PROTESTANT childhood had been layered over with many other experiences: secular, feminist, academic, urban, wife and mother. While I had become familiar with some Jewish traditions in Ames, at the time we moved to Brookline I didn't know very much about Israel. After all, I'd grown up knowing little Jewish history other than the Holocaust. I had always thought that questions concerning the U.S. relationship with Israel were really up to Jews to decide because they had a vested interest and knew its history. But my mind was changing. I was a citizen too and I wanted to know more, particularly about U.S. involvement. When I asked David questions about Israel, he always had quick answers tied to wars, like '67 or '73, and to land that had changed hands. But the gains of wars weren't what I wanted to know about. Rather, who were the people on each side? What were they fighting for? Who was David and who was Goliath? My questions caused me to realize that I needed to learn enough about Israel and Palestine's history so that I could answer these questions myself.

I remember the first eye-opening moment. I saw a map of the West Bank from the Oslo Accords II from 1995: Hundreds of small Palestinian cities and villages were a hodgepodge of disconnected islands entirely surrounded by the majority of land controlled by Israel. I take maps seriously. That's why I remember this one so clearly: How could a future State be disconnected like that? How could a plan like this lead to the two-state solution politicians had been talking about for decades? What I didn't know at that time is that what I was seeing was the developing structure of apartheid, a fracturing of connections between people and land. Had the Palestinians actually agreed to this? Yes, but as I would also find out later, Israel had reneged on plans for a two-state solution that were to follow the agreement.

The first time I asked David a question about Palestine, he seemed confused, as if there were no such thing, as if I'd invented the word. I told him I'd seen a map of Palestine. Even if there was no nation by that name, there were Palestinians, and a long history of the place. Three thousand years of history had passed between the 5th century BCE, when Herodotus described Palestine skirting the Mediterranean and the British Mandate of Palestine that introduced the borders we know today.

Then I naively asked David: Why would all those Palestinians have just left when Israel was founded? And he, who knew so much more than me about Jewish and Israeli history said: I don't know. They just left. Maybe another time he told me that they had left because they were told to by the Arab armies that had invaded at Israel's founding. (It took decades after 1948 to bust up that myth.) Israeli statehood caused the word "Arab" to be redefined, to refer to non-Jews who they were expelling and making into their enemy. But prior to the rise of nationalism, Jews who lived in Arab lands had referred to themselves, Muslims and Christians as "Arabs." Likewise, "Palestinian" had referred to any person born in or living in Palestine, regardless of their ethnic, cultural, or religious affiliations. But after Israel was founded, "Palestinian" came to exclusively refer to Arabs of the former Mandatory Palestine who were not Jewish. Those who did not become Palestinian Israeli citizens, who lived stateless in Gaza and the West Bank, and those who had become global refugees developed a distinctly Palestinian-Arab national identity.

I suppose my question about why the Palestinians left was prompted by some of those black-and-white photos of lines of Palestinian families carrying their belongings on a dirt road walking toward who-knows-where (much like the live-stream videos we are watching of today's genocide). Neither of us knew the word "Nakba" at that time. The word "Nakba," in Arabic meaning "catastrophe," refers to the violent displacement, dispossession of land, and the destruction of Palestinian society resulting from the establishment of the State of Israel.

David

MY MOTHER DIED IN 2002 and my father lived alone for a couple of years after that. It was a miserable time for him, especially after he totaled his car. (To his credit, though, he immediately resolved never to drive again.) Still, it took me quite a while to persuade him to move into the Goddard House, an assisted living place near us in Brookline. My father spent the last three years of his life there, and to my great surprise this turned out to be a wonderful chapter of my own. Before that my father and I had never been close. He was generous and reliable, but distant. He had tremendous energy, most of which he devoted to work. By profession he was a civil engineer, but his real love was math, which, after a long day job, he taught at night at Brooklyn Poly Tech. He didn't do it for the money, but because he liked it so much. Because he left for work before I got up in the morning, I didn't see him at all on those days. One of my few memories of being with him as a kid is when he would help me with my math homework. He could explain things simply and with wonderful patience. We would sit shoulder to shoulder at the dining room table, and I could tell he was glad to be there with me.

My dad had a temper, which was usually triggered by the stupidity of capitalism. I was largely spared from his anger since I was a good boy who did well in school and always did the few chores assigned to me. But I wasn't praised much either, at least not that I can remember, and I'm pretty sure he never once attended a soccer, basketball or baseball game in which I was playing. Things soured during my senior year of high-school (1968–69). Like a lot of old lefties, he hated the hedonism and excess of the counterculture of the 60's, and he didn't approve at all of my long hair or the way I was starting to dress. He wasn't crazy about me studying philosophy in college either. Not because there was no money in it, but because it was, for him, an escape from the real world and its struggles. He was deep down a practical man, a political man, while I was coming to love the ivory tower. After returning from

Israel in 1972, I never attended another protest rally. I think this may have disappointed him. We never lost touch, my father and I, but except for occasional family gatherings, we didn't see each other much for long stretches. This changed when our daughters were born. My parents adored them and Gina and I would regularly come to Connecticut. Often we'd leave the girls there and take a bus into New York, where we'd spend a few days enjoying all the stuff we couldn't do in Ames, Iowa.

My father was miserable during his first three months at the Goddard House, and he took to muttering "catastrophic" on a regular basis. We visited him almost every day during this period. And then he met Edith. Like my mother, she'd been a social worker and, like both my parents, she was an old-time Jewish activist who used to describe herself as a "real leftie." It turned out that she and my father had attended the same protest against the execution of the Rosenbergs in 1953. (Or so they surmised.) Although neither of them would have ever described it in these words, it was a match made in heaven, and it delighted me.

Edith was warm, funny, feisty and she occasionally wore black leather pants. She and my father quickly became inseparable and, to put it mildly, his spirits perked up. I would often arrive at the Goddard House just after they had finished dinner and had settled into the lounge. There they sat on a sofa, slumped into each other, and when I arrived my Dad was always happy to see me. To his cronies who shuffled by, and to whom I'd been introduced dozens of times, he'd say, "have you met my son?" And I'd feel great.

My father and I never had the intimate, revelatory conversations you might see in the movies, but we did spend more time together during those three years than we ever had. I took care of his financial affairs, made sure he hadn't left bills or soiled underwear on the floor of his room, drove him to the doctor and the dentist, brought him and Edith to our house for dinner. I never felt any of this was a burden since he was always appreciative and never once complained, at least about me. Whenever he had to go to the bathroom, which of course was often, he'd crack the same, slightly pointed joke. "You know what Socrates used to say? A wise man never misses the opportunity to urinate."

In the final three years of his life, my father, a restless man in perpetual conflict with a world he thought unjust, finally relaxed and became appreciative of the little he had left: me, my brother and his wife, Gina, his grandchildren, Edith and the waiter at the Goddard House who always made sure he got his vegetarian dinner. Only near the very end, when he was 93, did his memory start to deteriorate. He would occasionally lapse into the deep past. He once told me how much he liked being a soldier during World War II. I was surprised and asked why. "The physical discipline," he replied. I understood. He started to use Yiddish phrases, the language his parents spoke at home, which he had never done before. Once he told me he hated his father. By all accounts a taciturn and maybe even a cruel man, my grandfather was an Orthodox Jew who preferred the *schul* to his own home and family. Little wonder, I suppose, that my father became a devout atheist. But the most startling moment was when, out of nowhere, he said "I hate school." I was stunned by his use of the present tense. "Why?" I asked. "Because the teacher mispronounces my name." "Roochnik" is the English spelling of what an official on Ellis Island heard when my grandfather must have grunted, "Rucznik."

Gina

OUR FAMILY REGULARLY VISITED our parents, mine in Florida in the winter and Michigan in the summer, and David's, not too far away in Connecticut. Then my mother died suddenly of a heart attack just weeks after 9/11 and just days before my parents were about to move into assisted living. I felt very guilty about this because I had encouraged them to move. When I took my parents to lunch at the potential assisted living place, my Mom asked, where were they keeping the people who drooled? I admit we had a similar sense of humor based on blunt honesty. But her idea of assisted living came from nursing homes and she did not want to go. I was the one encouraging this decision and also the one who had moved away from the family. My father did not complain about anything and often told us how proud he was of his children. He moved into assisted living by himself and his death in 2003 followed the trajectory of the story he always told about his parents: After his mother died, he said that his father died of loneliness just two years later.

My parents had young children during the economic boom that followed WWII. From growing up on a farm and small town, they built their home in the suburbs. My father started a business by welding a trencher, I think it would be called, to a jeep so that he could connect the water lines from new homes to the street. By the time he retired in his late 50s, he was building streets in subdivisions and underground electrical infrastructure for lighting highways. He worked very hard, coming home sun-burned and dusty, so that his kids could have better lives. My mother became the bookkeeper that was crucial to their business, as well as homemaker for the family.

When I came home from college talking excitedly about feminism, my Mom let it slip that she wouldn't want to go to a female doctor. I said, but why not? At that time they probably had to do twice as well to get into medical school to become doctors and maybe they understand us better than men. My parents believed in gender equality, even though they thought men and women had different roles. They went out of their way to treat my brothers and me equally.

I like to think of my parents as Eisenhower Republicans probably because I have such admiration for his prescient fears about the military-industrial complex. But they didn't talk about politics much and probably always voted straight Republican. Above all, they believed in hard work and honesty. I think they would be appalled today by wealth that is earned, not from labor but from moving just money and numerals around. They were deeply self reliant. They didn't look for tax breaks, didn't even have a consultant do their taxes. They hardly ever went to doctors, usually just asking questions of my uncle who was a physician. They would have laughed at the thought of belonging to a gym.

Since my parents didn't depend on experts like people do today, they just expected to face whatever problems arose, their way, when they happened. By the time President Reagan came along, the media itself had replaced the face-to-face communication that they had grown up with. They got their news from the local newspaper and TV. When Reagan spoke to them on television, I think they trusted he was speaking honestly to them. They didn't question his policies. So when he spoke of getting rid of big government, their experience confirmed that anyone who was honest and responsible could have a good middle-class life without it. Certainly that was more true in the decades after WWII—if you were white. They defended racial equality but their understanding of it probably carried the idea, unfortunately, of separate but equal.

They visited us when we first moved to Brookline. My mom loved the front porch of our 1915 house where she could watch cars, pedestrians, cyclists, and skateboarders go by. When we were walking around downtown Boston together my father saw a guy sleeping on a bench. To my embarrassment he yelled to him, why don't you get a job? I wish my father had had the opportunity to broaden his understanding of the world so that his compassion extended beyond the people he knew.

David's mother died in 2002. In such a short time, we had lost three parents. We had often gone to Passover dinner at David's parents' house and Rosanna always found a way to tell the Passover story in a way that was just at the right level for our girls to appreciate. I also remember saying to David's mother once, when our girls were young and possibly when she and his father had just returned from an international trip, that maybe someday we could all go to Israel. David's mother looked at me with such questioning surprise. She didn't respond by saying, Yes, that would be good, or, No, I wouldn't want to. I only realized years later that I had assumed she would want our family to go to Israel when, in fact, she wasn't very interested. Another story I remember about Rosanna was when there was a lawsuit at Yale brought by Orthodox Jews who wanted special treatment so they would not have to live in mixed-sex housing as freshmen and sophomores. She was adamant that they should be treated no differently than all other students. She was a woman who believed in fairness, no matter one's religion.

After Rosanna's death David's father became the focus of our attention. Milton was not a cheery guy but he was totally devoted to the responsibilities of work and family. And he was the source of a love of math and of left-wing stories for our family. Had he been a communist? What protests had he and Rosanna attended in their youth? I learned that he had opposed the Vietnam War very early, well before the large protests. So when he moved into assisted living in Brookline and met Edith, his youthful and left-wing stories all came rushing back, particularly since Edith shared some of those stories. This gave David the chance once again to remind us of his left-wing credentials: He was a red diaper baby. When Edith and Milton came to our house for dinner the first time, she wore black leather pants and a big black-and-white button on her shirt with a fist that I thought stood for solidarity—with feminists, trade unionists, antifascists? She was eighty-some years old. I really admired her outspoken politics and we were very comforted to see Milton and Edith happily seated together when we visited.

David

IN 2007, OR THEREABOUTS, I read *My Promised Land: The Triumph and Tragedy of Israel* by Ari Shavit. I'm not sure why I read it. Perhaps it was because of a *New York Times* book review. In any case, it hit me hard. On the one hand, Shavit was deeply convinced that Israel was a triumph. No longer a vulnerable and despised minority, no longer defenseless victims of vicious pogroms, European Jews finally had a state of their own. Through phenomenal effort and resolve, they had built cities, resurrected the Hebrew language, planted fields, created industries, universities, hospitals, a vibrant culture and a powerful military. They had been fruitful and multiplied. But there was a dark side and Shavit, like others of the "new" Israeli historians at the time, did not (entirely) avert his gaze. In making a home for themselves those same European Jews displaced hundreds of thousands of Palestinians, and murdered many. The former victims had become victimizers. Although Shavit never wavered in his support of Zionism, a movement supporting an ethnonational state for Jews, he seemed to me to face up to this stark reality, and he helped me to start doing the same.

Gina

AT THE SAME TIME as David, I read *My Promised Land: The Triumph and Tragedy of Israel*. David talked about how impressive Israel's triumphs were. But Shavit also saw a dark side and suspected Israelis were in denial of what it had taken to achieve those triumphs. He introduced me to the violence of the Nakba. He reported the details of the 1948 expulsion of Palestinians from Lydda where Israeli soldiers set fire to the roofs of homes in the village and "the horrific massacre of men, women and children who found refuge in the city's small mosque." But he made it perfectly clear he thought that violence was the only choice: "They did the dirty, filthy work that enables my people, myself, my daughter and my sons to live." Why would he look back on Israel's ethnic cleansing and see it as the only way? Jews in the U.S. did not need to massacre people to be treated equally. (Admittedly, the U.S. had massacred indigenous people more than a century earlier). Who does Shavit blame for Israel's ethnic cleansing? The ayatollahs: "We'd prefer our Israel to be a sort of California, but the trouble is that this California of ours is surrounded by ayatollahs." Did he not know that California does not support Jewish supremacy nor steal others' land (anymore)? Shavit's book was the first to expose me to the dark history of Israel. I had believed Jews were the victims. But now I had to wonder how they could have thought their only choice for survival was ethnic cleansing just a few years after the Holocaust. Why would they think Jewish supremacy was their only hope for survival? What did the founders want? Was it really for Jews to live only among other Jews?

David

ANOTHER LANDMARK ON THE map of my past: the 2008 Israeli film *Waltz with Bashir*. Its writer/director was Ari Folman, who as a nineteen-year-old served in the IDF during the 1982 invasion of Lebanon. In this war Israel, together with its Christian allies (the Phalange), attacked the Palestine Liberation Organization's positions in southern Lebanon and laid siege to the capital Beirut. After the PLO negotiated a ceasefire and its leadership fled to Tunisia, a pro-Israeli Christian government led by Bashir Gemayel was installed. Within weeks, however, Gemayel was assassinated. In revenge, the Phalangists killed anywhere between 700 and 3000 Muslims, both Palestinian and Lebanese, in the neighborhood of Sabra and the refugee camp of Shatila. As the massacre unfolded, Israeli troops were positioned at the exits of the area to prevent the camp's residents from leaving and shot flares to illuminate Sabra and Shatila through that long and bloody night. A few months later, the Israeli Kahan Commission ruled that by doing nothing to stop the killings, the Israeli military was indirectly responsible for the events. This forced the Israeli defense minister Ariel Sharon to resign. (His political career, however, was anything but over and in 2001 he was elected as Prime Minister.)

In *Waltz With Bashir* Ari Folman recounts (in animated form) his attempt to retrieve and come to terms with his memories of fighting in Lebanon, for even though he was a kid who had no clue what was actually going on, he was one of the IDF soldiers who launched the flares into the sky so that the killers could see who they were shooting. It's a powerful movie and it made me furious. I remember saying—to whom I do not know—that Sharon must be tried as a war criminal.

What this, as well as my positive reaction to Shavit's book, means is that by 2008 I was becoming critical of Israel. The occupation of the West Bank and Gaza could not, I had come to believe, be justified. (Israel withdrew from Gaza in 2006, but continued to maintain a blockade and control what and who went in or out.)

Nonetheless, the government steadily expanded Jewish settlements on the West Bank and the occupation became ever more entrenched. An Israeli graduate student, himself a critic of his own country, gave me a book that also made a big impression on me: David Grossman's *Yellow Wind* (1988). Written by one of Israel's greatest novelists, it is a devastating account of what life is actually like for Palestinians living in refugee camps on the West Bank, and how much has been taken away from them.

Despite the hardening of my stance on Israel, and the suspicions brewing in my mind concerning the repeated invocation of the Holocaust to defend its existence, I didn't give either issue a great deal of thought. I was more engaged by my own country's invasions of Afghanistan and Iraq, wars that turned out to be variations on the old awful theme of Vietnam. And, of course, I was still preoccupied with my family and writing books. Gina's story was quite different.

Gina

I FIRST HEARD ABOUT Jewish Voice for Peace about 2012. I wanted Jewish friends who were asking the same questions as me about Israel. Was that to confirm that I wasn't antisemitic? Or was it based on the idea that Jews better understood issues related to Israel? I don't know. I attended a few meetings at the Community Church in Boston but I didn't really get to know anyone right away. It was the national JVP with this title bar on its website—Israelis and Palestinians. Two Peoples, One Future—that offered me resources. I learned that JVP was founded by three UC Berkeley undergraduate Jewish women many years earlier. JVP introduced me to Zionism and Jewish opposition to it. A short animated video illustrated the history of Israel-Palestine. Most of all, what benefited me were the films, videos, and books listed there, particularly by Miko Peled, Shlomo Sand, and Ilan Pappe.

I learned from Miko Peled, whose father was a General in the '67 War and later became critical of Israeli policies, that his mother had been offered a beautiful home in Jerusalem in 1948 because his father had been an officer in what Israelis call the War of Independence and Palestinians call the Nakba. But she refused to take a Palestinian family's stolen home when its family had been forced to live in a refugee camp rather than on the land their ancestors had inhabited for centuries. She was Jewish and from a military family, yet she refused to partake in the dispossession of Palestinians. I was also struck by the fact that Jerusalem, where Miko Peled grew up, was such a segregated city that he never got to know Palestinians until he moved to California in midlife. How could an Israeli, brought up in that small country, have never met a Palestinian? Today, following the construction of apartheid with its separate roads and checkpoints, Israelis are even less likely to interact with stateless Palestinians.

I read *The Invention of the Jewish People* (2009) when our family was visiting our daughter, on a foggy Cannon Beach in Oregon in 2016. Shlomo Sand was asking questions about Jewish identity that I had been wondering about for years. Sand was a child of the 1950s, brought up at a time when he describes that Jewish history taught that the Jews were a pure people from ancient time to the present, including Biblical heroes who had promised the land of Israel to the Jews. Being a descendent of the ancient Jewish people became a part of his self-identity until he began to ask questions. Who would think that today's Greeks are descended from Aristotle or Italians from Caesar? Nevertheless Jewish Israelis have believed their ancestors "wandered in exile for nearly two thousand years and yet, despite this prolonged stay among the gentiles, managed to avoid integration with, or assimilation into, them." Then, at the end of the 19th century, fortuitously, they returned to their ancient homeland?

Sand begins his great historical journey by questioning "the exile," the notion that the Romans expelled the Jews en masse from Palestine. For it is upon exile that the idea of return is built. How could they have maintained their biological distinctness in a vast dispersion to the periphery of the Christian world? Sand documents Jewish proselytizing and centuries of conversions in the remote communities where they lived: Yemen, Morocco, Spain, Germany, Poland and remote Russia.

Sand closes his work by surveying the role eugenics, an idea that was prominent among early Zionists, played in the development of Jewish identity. "Nathan Birnbaum, who coined the term "Zionist" in 1890, believed that neither culture nor language, but only biology, could explain the existence of the Jewish nation." Yet in genetic studies, undertaken since cracking the human genome and by the time of his book's publication, "no research had found unique and unifying characteristics of Jewish heredity based on a random sampling whose ethnic origin is unknown in advance."

Israeli historian Ilan Pappe's 2006 book, *The Ethnic Cleansing of Palestine,* details Israel's role in the Nakba, and the Zionist master plan for ethnic cleansing—designated by international law as a crime against humanity. Pappe challenges the Israeli narrative that Palestinians had left their homes in droves in 1948 because Arab armies had told them to because they were planning to attack the new State of Israel. Instead, Pappe's research transforms Israel from victim to perpetrator of war by documenting Ben Gurion's Plan D for the ethnic cleansing of Palestinians. In 1938, before Ben Gurion became Israel's first Prime Minister, he said, "I am for compulsory transfer. I do not see anything immoral in it." He knew Palestinians would not leave their land otherwise. Although Zionists had long debated what kind of state Israel could be, the Plan confirmed their decision for an exclusively Jewish State rather than a Jewish homeland. Plan D called for the destruction of both rural villages and urban neighborhoods and was finalized on March 10, 1948. The military mission took six months to complete after which "more than half of Palestine's native population, close to 800,000 people, had been uprooted, 531 villages had been destroyed, and eleven urban neighborhoods emptied of their inhabitants."

Under the 1950 Law of Return, the Jewish State offered citizenship to Jews from anywhere in the world, although most choose not to live in Israel. But the Palestinians who were expelled in 1948 and dispossessed of their property, to this day have no right of return. (Along with robbing Palestinians of their land, their homes, their furniture, their belongings and their bank accounts, the documentary film by Israeli-Dutch filmmaker Benny Brunner, *The Great Book Robbery* (2007–2012), shows how Israel even methodically robbed them of their books—tens of thousands of books, privately and then by the State as "Abandoned Property" in 1948. The film's photo documentation was the first I had seen of what neighborhoods had looked like emptied of Palestinians, wrapped in spiral topped fencing, in places such as West Jerusalem.)

Israeli "new historians" in the 1980s had broadly challenged the Zionist narrative of what happened in 1948 but avoided calling out ethnic cleansing before Pappe's 2006 book. But the victims had long had evidence. To acknowledge earlier, largely unknown sources Pappe cited some. In the 1970s, Palestinian historians, particularly Walid Khalidi, had collected memories and photographed sites of more than four hundred Palestinian villages that were destroyed or "depopulated" in *All That Remains: The*

Palestinian Villages Occupied and Depopulated by Israel in 1948 (1992). In 1987 Michael Palumbo published *The Palestinian Catastrophe* citing newly discovered archival documents that exposed Ben-Gurion's plans as well as documenting the memories of Palestinian refugees and Western observers.

Pappe's book had turned my thinking around and altered the global conversation. A book written by Rashid Khalidi, fourteen years after Pappe's and five decades after his cousin Walid's research, extended the length of Israel's wars to *The Hundred Years' War on Palestine: A History of Settler Colonialism and Resistance, 1917–2017* (2020). Yet the Nakba remains largely unspoken. Would it be unfair to say that Israel and its U.S. lobby have for all these decades strong-armed their victimhood narrative on us to overwhelm the truth?

I found it difficult not to tell David what I was learning about Israel. When I did, he was often defensive. Was he more tied to Israel than either he or I had thought? David is conflict averse. He is very sensitive to criticism. He has a very quick, sometimes angry response to being questioned, as if he's been accused of being irresponsible. I've learned to approach change slowly because he usually comes around, sometimes in minutes, sometimes longer. In one of our heated conversations he said that my focus on Israel must be about him. Why else would I be so interested in Israeli history except for knowing him?

It's true that knowing David, being introduced to some Jewish traditions, and having Jewish friends who supported equal rights offered me the agency I needed to speak about Palestine and Israel's intertwined histories. But to David's question I said no. It's not about you. It's about me feeling the bitterness of having been deceived: deceived by Israeli propaganda, deceived by U.S. journalists and politicians, deceived by the U.S. government. Did the State Department and Congress (and do they still) really not know Israel's history?

David

FOR NEARLY TWENTY YEARS I got together with a group of friends on almost every Sunday afternoon in the Fall and Winter to watch the New England Patriots play football. With Tom Brady at quarterback, and Bill Belichick as the coach, it was the golden age for us fans, and anything less than a victory in the Super Bowl, which we achieved six times, meant the season was a disappointment. (It's probably no coincidence that I retired from fanhood in 2019, the year Brady left the team.)

I'd been a sports fan since I was kid, but with those friends and that wonderful team this was far and away the most fun I'd ever had watching games. We'd all bring food and beer, and, cheering in joy or screaming in anger or just laughing at each other's stupidity, we'd make a lot of noise. I especially remember one moment. Julian Edelman, a terrific receiver and one of the few professional football players who was Jewish, made a spectacular catch. I reminded my friends, loudly I'm sure, that he was Jewish and then said something like, "that's my man! Yeshiva University, class of 5735!" It got a big laugh, and I was pleased with myself.

The truth is, though, someone else once made a better and much deeper joke. After a long struggle with cancer, his wife had recently died. He didn't show up for several Sundays, but finally he rejoined us. We were glad. We truly liked and cared about each other. Anyway, the game that day turned out badly for the Patriots, who lost by a wide margin. Not surprisingly, my friend was subdued and quiet for most of the game, but after one particularly terrible play on our part, he stood up and yelled at the television, "you assholes! Don't you know I'm in mourning?"

Gina

WHEN THE NEW ENGLAND Patriots were winning Super Bowls, David had a special relationship with Julian Edelman, Patriots' star football player. But it's hard for me to explain what is special about it. David has mentioned the fact that Edelman is Jewish many times. I've been wondering what that might mean. That because David's parents were Jewish both he and Edelman are from the same blood line? That they have the same values? Or that they share 3,000 years of history?

David doesn't know Julian Edelman. I doubt they will ever meet. But you'd think they have a deep connection. If they do it is certainly one-way. I don't think Edelman tells his friends that he knows David nor any of the Jewish spectators who might also identify him as one of them.

David doesn't exactly say he is friends with Edelman but he had a men-friends' Patriots-watching group that used to get together to share, occasionally defeat, and more often victory (before they tired of football and the Patriots). None of the group were Jewish except David and none were religious. I joined them a few times when they met at our house. David mentioned that Edelman was Jewish at least once, perhaps several times, while the group was watching a game. What might David's friends have thought when he mentioned Edelman's Jewishness? Might they have wished they were Jewish so they could have this special relationship with Edelman too? Certainly not. It was a joke.

David has a good sense of humor. It is often based on saying the opposite of what is expected and then repeating it (many times). The guys in the football group don't care whether Edelman is Jewish or not, in fact neither does David really, which is why it is unexpected. And funny. But why is it funny? Is it because it is so obvious that it doesn't mean a thing to say that both he and Julian are Jewish? Or does it actually mean something? If so, what? That they might both have relatives in New York? Or that they might both have grandparents who came from Russia? Or that they have relatives who survived or died in the Holocaust? That's not funny.

Is saying Edelman is Jewish funny because only David can say it? Imagine if one of the other guys, say whose parents were Methodists, said, "Did you know Julian Edelman is Jewish?" That question would land with a thud. And probably raise questions. What are Methodists doing identifying Jews? It's an insider question to ask, Did you know so-and-so is Jewish?, so maybe that's why it's funny.

A friend of mine who is Jewish says that when he was growing up Jews were thought not to be athletic so he thinks that may be the reason David would say it. I wouldn't have thought of that since David himself is very athletic.

What if one of the guys said "Did you know that (wide receiver coach) Chad O'Shea is Catholic?" It's just not funny. Especially since O'Shea is seriously religious. Could David's question be funny only because it suggests that two people who know nothing about one another share some deep religious history, especially when David is not religious? Would it have been funny prior to WWII? I don't think so. Would it have been funny before the '67 War? I don't think so. Why is it funny now?

How funny is this: Did you know Julian Edelman is Christian? That doesn't strike a funny bone. But in fact, according to the Patriots' media office, Edelman was raised as a Christian, and his ancestry includes Greek, English, Scottish, Irish, Ashkenazi Jewish, and German. Wikipedia says that it was Edelman's paternal great-grandfather, Harry Edelman, who was Jewish. So that might make Edelman 1/16th Jewish, if he had proof his great-great-grandmother was Jewish. But Wikipedia also reveals that Edelman had experienced what he described as an awakening. During an interview in December 2013, Edelman stated that he identified as Jewish and has become more attuned to the religion and history.

In 2014 he wore an Israeli-American flag pin on his hat during a game at Gillette Stadium. I've never seen such a pin but apparently you can buy them online from church suppliers. These would be big sellers to Christian Zionists, (the voting base of Trump and supporters of Netanyahu), who believe that the State of Israel is a fulfillment of Biblical prophecy. That's not funny.

David

THE MORE SHE READ about what Israel had done, and was doing, to the Palestinians, the more disturbed Gina became. She simply could not understand why Americans, and not just Jews, so totally supported it. For most of her life what she had heard from friends and the media was the refrain, Jews-are-victims, Jews-are-victims, Jews-are-victims, and when she started to learn how terribly Israel had victimized the Palestinians she felt deceived, cheated, lied to, and this, more than anything else, made her mad. And then there was the way in which, as she saw it, Jews, in a variety of ways, count themselves as somehow exceptional. This offended her, for she has a deep, and totally authentic, conviction that human beings are fundamentally equal.

Israel and the Jews had come to figure very prominently in her life, and it was often a topic of our conversations. Even though these often puzzled, and sometimes annoyed me, and they were becoming quite repetitive, I was impressed by the way ideas, political ones, were driving her. The question that regularly pulled me up short, however, was still, why did those Jews who wouldn't dream of stepping foot inside a synagogue, and whose spouses weren't Jewish, continue to identify themselves as members of the tribe? Why did their eyes, like mine, linger on Jewish names in the newspaper? What were they hoping to find?

I once went to the movies with my friends Mike and Tina. It was a documentary about the history of the blues in Chicago, and it put special emphasis on those white teenagers from the suburbs—Mike Bloomfield, Paul Butterfield, Barry Goldberg, Harvey Mandel, Corky Siegel—who ventured to the South Side where they listened to, and learned from, their African-American heroes: Muddy Waters and Howlin' Wolf. When it was over Tina, who is Jewish (Mike is not), rushed up to me. She could barely contain her excitement. "They're all Jewish!" she exclaimed, her eyes wide in amazement. Somewhat befuddled, I was tempted to tell her Paul

Butterfield wasn't, but I kept that to myself. Instead, I muttered something like "people born in pain."

Sometimes when Gina would talk about "Jewish exceptionalism" or rant about the power of AIPAC, I would shudder. Of course, there were times when I couldn't help but wonder if some of her growing anger was directed not at Israel, but at me.

Gina

In 2016, when I watched the documentary film *The Occupation of the American Mind*, I took pages of notes to remind myself again of what happened at Israel's founding. In 1947 the UN Partition Plan recommended the creation of independent but economically linked Arab and Jewish States. The proposed Jewish State, which by that time had 1/3 of the population and owned only 7.4% of the land, was given 56% of the land while the Palestinians, who were 2/3 of the population and possessed more than 90% of historic Palestine, were given 44%. Arab leaders rejected these unreasonable terms. By February 1948, the U.S. administration had already concluded that the UN Partition Plan would not bring peace; instead, more bloodshed. It twice offered alternatives, such as a five-year trusteeship and a three-month ceasefire, but both were immediately rejected by Zionist leadership. In the spring of 1948 Zionists leaders declared Israel a state on the proposed border anyway, triggering the first of Israel's wars against Palestinians. Israel's victory meant taking even more land so that by armistice day in 1949 Israel took control of 75% of the land, Palestinians 22%.

Israelis knew that this injustice would eventually come to light as would their illegal occupation and building of settlements following the 1967 War. How could Israel keep American support despite the fact that the majority of Americans have always opposed illegal occupation and settlements? The film showed how Israeli lobbies manipulated the American media and Congress by hiring troubleshooters from well-funded public relations firms to change the conversation. The Israel Project hired conservative pollster and rebranding expert Frank Lunz to reframe the discourse. Since both the occupation and the settlements have consistently created sympathy for Palestinians from Americans, Lunz proposed avoiding those terms in his 2009 report, The Global Language Dictionary.

What word would scare Americans into acquiescence with Israel? Terror. Lunz advised talking about terror rather than territory, security rather than peace. Following his publication, news reports repeatedly referred to Palestinians as terrorists. Years later we are all familiar with Israeli officials describing those who disagree with their policies as terrorists and repeatedly using the word "security" to suggest they are the vulnerable ones rather than the aggressors. While no definition of "terrorism" is universally agreed upon, it broadly applies to violence against ordinary people to achieve political goals. Today those who dare oppose U.S. policy on Israel have been called terrorists.

David

For years Gina has repeatedly asked a question: why do so many Americans identify as Jewish even though they are not the least bit religious? She herself wouldn't dream of identifying as Christian precisely because she is not the least bit religious. Why, then, would someone like me feel a bond to a tribe of which he was never really a member? This question used to stump me. Perhaps because, even though I had never met one, I actually feared that Cossacks were a permanent possibility. Or perhaps my stay on Kfar HaNassi gave me a taste of the land that I could not forget. Was it my admiration for my grandfather, who loved both Israel and being Jewish, or my brief stint at Ramaz that had forged the connection? Or were my own feelings as mysterious as Ruth's tears were on Kfar HaNassi back in 1971, when she began to weep at the sheer improbability of a Jew living in Israel after centuries of exile?

It was not only Gina's question that stumped me. It was also the fact that she not only asked it, but seemed preoccupied by it.

Gina

EVEN THOUGH FOR YEARS David had told me that I had no reason to worry about being accused of antisemitism, I told him that the questions I was now asking about Israel might be considered by some people to be so. I even wondered whether I could say some of the things I was thinking to him. I was shocked when I compared what I'd thought of the Israeli project in previous decades—taking care of Jewish refugees and working toward a two-state solution—to what I was learning about it now. I was afraid to think Jews were not as innocent as I'd imagined. I was also beginning to fear that this "mixed marriage" of ours was more vulnerable than I'd thought.

I had much catching up to do. I was pretty surprised to learn that most early Jewish Zionists were not religious. It hadn't surprised me that most of my friends who identified themselves as Jewish were not religious. But the founders of Israel? I could understand why Zionists who had fled pogroms and become steeped in Western culture wanted to live free of religion but why would they then found a nation based on a religion? Or was it European antisemitism itself that made them Jewish?

Something else hit me: The Palestinians had nothing to do with the Holocaust. I remember saying this to David. He said that some Ottoman leaders supported Germany, without providing details. So what? Many Arab intellectuals opposed Nazism and some Zionists worked with the Nazi Party after the Kristallnacht in 1938. The question remains: Why were the Palestinians being punished rather than Western countries? Was it not in Christian Europe where antisemitism had thrived and from where Jews had to escape? Was it not the British empire's and Balfour's antisemitism that supported the Zionists' settler colonial project? Hadn't European countries debated for centuries The Jewish Question regarding the status of their unwelcome Jewish minorities?

Yet we have been led to think that it is the Arab world that is intolerant and timelessly tribal. In an episode of Jacobin Radio's podcast *The Dig*, which David and I both enjoy, Daniel Denvir talked with historian Ussama Makdisi about his book, *Age of Co-existence: The Ecumenical Frame and the Making of the Modern Arab World* (2021). Makdisi described the Ottoman government, an Islamic caliphate up until the mid-nineteenth century of which Palestine was part, as "a multiethnic, multireligious, multilinguistic empire that didn't presume that everyone was the same, didn't try to make everyone to one religion, didn't try to convert everybody, didn't make everyone speak the same language." There was no Jewish Question in the Ottoman world.

I hadn't even understood before this time that "the Jewish State" meant discriminating against everyone who was not Jewish. Early Zionists who dreamed of a Jewish State aspired to control land from the river to the sea, and beyond, as illustrated in the World Zionist Organisation 1919 map where a future Jewish state covered all of Palestine and extended into Transjordan, Egypt, Saudi Arabia, Syria, and Lebanon.

Four decades after Israel's 1967 victory in the Six Day War, I learned why this war was such a landmark. The Zionists' dream had surfaced and Israel took possession of Mandatory Palestine from the river to the sea. But this created more problems. For one, equal numbers of Jews and Palestinians lived from the river to the sea. How would Jews maintain the majority status that kept them in power? For another, occupying powers have responsibilities to the people living there. With responsibilities to millions of non-Jewish people, ethnic cleansing was (presumably) no longer an option. What then? Apartheid.

Israel's first step towards institutionalizing apartheid was achieved through laws that discriminated against Palestinians. They were divided into three geographic groups: Palestinians living in Israel were citizens without the advantages of being Jewish nationals, in East Jerusalem they were non-citizens identified as "residents," and those in the occupied territories, Gaza and the West Bank, were non-citizens who lived under military rule. The physical construction of apartheid followed by refining segregation with separation walls, separate road systems, hundreds of check-points and other obstacles, as well as restrictions on travel and access to water, plus high-tech surveillance, and much more.

Israel's is the longest occupation in modern history. The occupation and the construction of apartheid are illegal under international law. Together they have, for all practical purposes, destroyed the possibility of a two-state solution. The Palestinians' right to self-determination is internationally recognized. The subsequent creation of settlements is illegal under international law. Yet Israel disregards international law. And so does the U.S.

David

GINA'S CRITIQUE OF ISRAEL was steadily becoming more radical than my own, for hers targeted not only the occupation or Benjamin Netanyahu, but Zionism itself. She was convinced that something was rotten at Israel's core. Far from being little Davids who had defeated Arab Goliaths in 1948, the well-armed Zionists had displaced hundreds of thousands of innocent people from their homes, slaughtering many in the process. By her lights, Israel was first and foremost a settler colonial power. For a long time I recoiled at this accusation. Yes, I agreed, as Israeli historians (like Benny Morris) had verified, the Zionists had violently expelled Palestinians from their land, and so in this sense it was fair to compare what Israel was doing to what the British had done (on such a massive scale). But there was, I insisted, a fundamental difference. The Brits had an empire and their goal was to make it bigger and themselves richer. The European Jews? They didn't even have a state. For centuries they'd been strangers, persecuted, despised and vulnerable in a Christian world, and their goal was not to amass wealth or power, but to survive as a people. The early Zionists were convinced this would be impossible in Europe, and Hitler proved them right. Post-Holocaust Zionists were fiercely determined to carve a homeland for themselves in Palestine by any means necessary, even if this meant doing terrible things to the people who were already there.

I wanted Gina to realize that, like Ari Shavit, she could hold two ideas at once. Yes, the Jews were fighting for their survival. Yes, the Jews violently expelled the Palestinians who lived there before they arrived. But her single-minded conviction never wavered. The Zionist project was colonialism and deserved to be condemned. Full stop.

Gina

OUR CONVERSATIONS WERE GETTING to be downright adversarial as I learned more about what Israel had been up to for so long. There have been many violent and unjust nations during my lifetime, including the U.S., but none more duplicitous than Israel. It has marketed Jewish victimhood to the world while it has continued the occupation, subverted the two-state solution, built settlements and developed a powerful military with U.S. tax dollars. This made me furious. Israel has been so duplicitous that I will never again believe anything their government reports without an independent investigation for verification. Nevertheless I had to stop complaining to David about Israel's latest attacks while we read the newspaper in the morning. He wasn't responsible for them. I would not conflate David nor all Jews and Israelis with Israel. I knew many Jews who believed that both Israel's and Palestinians' liberation would only come about through equality and freedom for all people. My accusations needed to be directed toward Zionists.

John Mearsheimer and Stephen Walt wrote *The Israel Lobby and U.S. Foreign Policy*, (2006), to make the argument that unwavering U.S. support for Israel derives not from shared strategic interests but largely from the influence of the Israel Lobby. (David often refers to the pro-Israel lobby. Does he think there's an anti-Israel lobby?) It was shocking 15 years ago even to see the words "Israel Lobby" in print for there seemed to be an unwritten law that one should not utter that phrase. Sure enough, Mearsheimer and Walt were widely accused of antisemitism, and these words, the Israel Lobby, even put David on edge. (Nevertheless, the Lobby has become so much more powerful now that in the 2024 elections, it was only mildly surprising to read that the American Israel Public Affairs Committee (AIPAC), one of the most powerful of Israel lobbies, would spend $100 million to fund candidates—even ones that supported the insurrection against the election outcome—so long as they also supported Israel. I certainly wouldn't dare to accuse AIPAC of dual loyalty for that would be a trope.)

When former President Jimmy Carter published *Palestine: Peace Not Apartheid*, (2006) he was attacked by the Anti-Defamation League (ADL), Nancy Pelosi, Bill Clinton, and many more, as well as in a review in the *New York Times*. Only years later when the U.N. concluded that conditions in Israel constituted apartheid in 2017, and Human Rights Watch did the same, were we less silenced from talking about Israel's demographic engineering that has fractured and dominated the Palestinian people.

I was puzzled for decades when I repeatedly heard Israeli officials say that they had no one to negotiate with. What did they mean? Wasn't it obvious who they needed to negotiate with? They also often said that Palestinians had to accept Israel's "right to exist." (Apparently so do Americans. In 2023, the U.S. House affirmed Israel's "right to exist" by a vote of 412–1. But Peter Beinart tells us in a *New York Times* Op-Ed that "States Don't Have a Right to Exist. People Do.") Agreeing to Israel's right to exist essentially means accepting Jewish supremacy. In addition to demanding its right to exist, Israel is unwilling to negotiate about anything that happened before 1967. After decades of "peace processes" it has become pretty clear that Israel chooses more domination, more military power, more destruction and will not negotiate with anyone who disagrees with the Jewish State. Israel has transformed "peace processes" into land grabs, taking additional land in every one of them, further foreclosing the possibility of a two-state solution.

In President Obama's final days in office I remember when he led support for the United States' only abstention on a UN Security Council resolution demanding an end to Israeli settlements on Palestinian territory. Though U.S. policy and international law have long recognized the illegality of building settlements on occupied land, Obama was the first to openly oppose them. The U.S. abstention allowed the resolution to pass easily. Since then, U.S. presidents have just looked the other way. (Before October 7, Israel had moved more than 700,000 illegal settlers into the occupied

West Bank. Five days after former President Trump's re-election, the Israeli foreign minister announced plans to annex the entire West Bank. Weeks later Israeli tanks entered the West Bank.)

I learned about "mowing the grass," what Israel officially called its military policy in Gaza, both from the news and from writers I have worked with there who had experienced it directly. A crude and cruel metaphor, mowing the grass implies Palestinians need to be regularly mown down to maintain control of them. Gaza was regularly bombed by Israel in 2006, 2012, 2014, 2018, and 2021. In Israel's 2014 assault on Gaza, the ratio of Palestinian deaths to Israelis was 32:1. Was Israel defending itself? An Israeli friend who visited us in 2018 told us of how his family had to go into the stairwell at times for fear of missile attacks. But I found it difficult to sympathize with going to a stairwell compared to being serially bombed with support from the largest military in the world.

Before I quit Facebook in 2014, I posted a *New York Times* photo that David had forwarded to me of young Israelis sitting on couches on a hilltop, with cans littering the ground, watching bombs drop on Gaza as if it were entertainment. A friend of my daughter's emailed me to say I was antisemitic for posting it.

Even though international law gives occupied peoples the right to armed resistance, Palestinians have a long history of nonviolent resistance. In recent decades, two stand out: the Great March of Return and BDS, a Palestinian-led nonviolent movement to Boycott, Divest, Sanction Israel that was founded in 2005. Designed to pressure Israel to meet its obligations under international law, the fact that the movement has become global has led Israel to consider BDS a "strategic threat," and spend millions to promote the view that BDS is antisemitic.

Every Friday for more than a year, beginning in 2018, protestors gathered peacefully for the Great March of Return. From inside the border fence that surrounds Gaza, Palestinians demanded an end to the 12-year-long Israeli blockade and the right to return to their ancestors' homes confiscated by Israel in 1948. During the demonstrations, Israeli soldiers killed 266 people, many of whom were providing medical assistance, and injured almost 30,000 others, often by shooting them in their knees. (Were IDF soldiers imitating the punishment meted out by Northern Ireland paramilitary groups chronicled by the Irish hip hop band so-named Kneecap who now criticize Israel's genocide?) Survivors in Gaza walking with crutches remind Palestinians every day of Israel's failure to recognize nonviolence. The failure to support nonviolent resistance of both BDS and the Great March by the U.S. and Israel was surely not lost on Hamas.

Understanding "mowing the grass" had also coincided with me coming to understand that Gaza was essentially an outdoor prison replete with spiral prison fencing and requiring permits to leave that were rarely approved by Israel. Before they were prisoners, Gazans were "refugees" whose homes in Palestine were stolen in 1948. From inside Gaza some refugees can even see their former homes. (What I hadn't learned about "mowing the grass" until after October 7 was the history of Netanyahu's support for Hamas so that Israel would not have to take responsibility for its occupation.)

David

As Gina became more politically active—attending demonstrations nearly weekly with other members of Jewish Voice for Peace, regularly writing letters to *The Boston Globe,* participating in Zoom meetings and seminars—her rhetoric at home heated up, sometimes to the point of rage. She would rant at the streams of propaganda designed to convince the world that any criticism of Israel was tantamount to antisemitism. For most of her life, she had unreflectively assumed that Jews, as victims, deserved a state of their own, and the only reason the Arabs did not welcome them to Palestine was their hatred. As she learned how much of the real story the Zionists had buried, she became increasingly indignant. For her one fact was as overwhelming as it was straightforward: there were people already living in Palestine when the European Jews arrived and, from the beginning, the Zionists were determined to take their land. Israel was expanding its settlements on the West Bank, turning Gaza into a prison, and inflicting misery upon millions of innocent Palestinians who wanted nothing more than the chance to live decent lives on their own terms. And America helped Zionists do it.

I could not deny much of what she was saying, but the way she would say it—blunt, indignant, self-righteous—often put me on edge.

Gina

I HADN'T REALLY GOTTEN to know people from JVP until I joined activities with the Boston chapter in 2016. Meeting them I learned that many of the local Jewish supporters of Palestinian rights, even some whose parents suffered in the Holocaust, had become critical of Israeli policies because, when they traveled to Israel, they visited the West Bank and had seen first hand how the occupation daily destroys the lives of Palestinians.

The first local activity I participated in was the 5K Walk for Water, along the Charles River in Cambridge. On the Walk for Water I got to know people in JVP Boston and their coalition with the Alliance for Water Justice in Palestine and 1for3.org, an organization focused on water, food, health, and education in UN-run refugee camps in the West Bank. In violation of international law, the water resources in Palestine are fully controlled by Israel, including aquifers that originate in the West Bank.

That day I met Palestinians for the first time: Nidal Al-Azraq, the Executive Director of 1for3 and his family. Nidal is a Palestinian refugee born and raised in the Aida refugee camp in Bethlehem, West Bank, Palestine, now living in Massachusetts. (In November, 2024, a local Cambridge architect who volunteered to help 1for3, was pushed to the street at gunpoint by two IDF soldiers when he visited the camp to check on the progress of building projects he was working on there. He experienced only a tiny bit of the aggression Palestinians face in the West Bank, which include raids, detentions, beatings, killings, and the destruction of homes that leave them in a permanent state of instability.)

To take the 5K Walk, I had to miss having lunch with David and his cousin. Seeing her later, after she knew I had been walking in support of Palestinians, she asked me what I thought the solution was. I shrugged my shoulders and said, a binational state? She seemed dissatisfied. Her husband had once mentioned that Labour Party leader Jeremy Corbyn was antisemitic. I was surprised. I told him that's not what I had thought. My understanding was that antisemitism had been weaponized by forces hostile to Corbyn. Nevertheless, we enjoy getting together with David's cousins but I sense myself an outsider, the one who can't really understand Israel.

Although I had worked with a neighborhood group supporting Congressman Joe Kennedy's re-election campaign in earlier years (2013–2021), with JVP Boston I attended protests of his support for Israel's regular bombing of Gaza. There I met Eve Spangler and read her book, *Understanding Israel/Palestine: Race, Nation, and Human Rights in the Conflict*. It explained why Israel can't control the land, be a Jewish state, *and* be democratic. (In 2022, Jake Auchincloss was elected to Congress following Kennedy's term. Auchincloss ran opposing "forever wars," but he has been an avid supporter of Israel's ongoing ethnic cleansing. JVP Boston and others have been protesting at his office in Newton nearly every week since he was elected.)

The news of George Floyd's murder on May 25, 2020, and the enormous protests in the U.S. about police brutality that followed, sped around the world. Palestinians tweeted advice to protesters. Protesters waved Palestinian flags. In the decades since the civil rights movement, many Black and Palestinian activists have shared their struggle against racism, including their opposition to Zionism. Taqi Spateen, a well known Palestinian painter and graffiti artist, was inspired to paint a mural of Floyd in the middle of the night on the Israeli Separation Wall in Bethlehem in the occupied West Bank. Rather than signing his name, Spateen painted the words: "I can't breathe. I want justice, not O_2."

We live in a two-family house with a large front porch close to the sidewalk. Each couple in our two-family house comes from both Jewish and Christian backgrounds. After Human Rights Watch reported in 2021 that Israel was guilty of the crime of apartheid, we attached a JVP bumper sticker to the rocking chair, centered between our two front doors, that said: APARTHEID ISN'T KOSHER. It was ripped off twice in the first weeks so I reported it to the police. I don't think the officer who wrote up the incident understood what it meant. He said there were reports of teenage vandals. I securely attached the bumper sticker to a metal plate where it has remained. Early on a neighbor asked if it had to do with South Africa. I said no, the kosher part implies it's about Israel.

I remember well the day in 2021 when Mike Pompeo, as Trump's Director of the CIA, went to the West Bank to celebrate a new illegal settlement. In desperation, I ordered a stack of FREE PALESTINE flag pins. I have worn one on my coat nearly every day since and given many away. To me the button says I will not be silenced. Wearing it has made me more aware of how people look at me and even changed my behavior. I am friendlier wearing it because I feel like I'm representing something larger than myself. More than a hundred strangers in my town have quietly told me they like my pin. Many were cashiers at places I patronize who may have felt like they shouldn't speak about politics at work. Many were young people just walking down the street. I even wear it to the synagogue a block from my house where I go each week to a modern dance class. Like a bank, there is always a guard there. He sees my pin, smiles and says good morning.

David

ONE STORY IN PARTICULAR spoke deeply to Gina, who's a landscape architect, and she shared it with me. After expelling some 700,000 Palestinians, the Zionists proceeded to destroy what remained of their villages. To cover up their dirty work, they planted trees atop what had been homes. These forests then became symbols of Jewish triumph. In the Zionist story, which I myself had somehow imbibed, Palestine had been a wasteland, over-grazed by goats, belonging to and cared for by no one until the Jews arrived from Europe and lovingly brought the ancient land back to life. That their forests grew over the ruins of villages they had destroyed was not mentioned. Strikingly, the trees planted were mostly pines, which in that part of the world, she told me, are not a native species.

The story upset me. I'd seen those trees.

A vague memory: as a kid I contributed a few dollars and bought a tree in Israel. Or perhaps one was purchased in my name.

A clear memory: in addition to courses in Philosophy, I used to teach Ancient Greek at Iowa State (which had no classics department). Most of my students were Christians who wanted to read the New Testament in Greek. One was a nun. I think her name was Glenda. At the beginning of the semester in January she handed me an envelope. In it was a document stating that a tree had been planted in Israel in my name. She explained that she had spent the winter break there. And then she looked me in the eye and said, firmly but with no anger, she wanted me to know she was supportive of the Palestinian cause. Of course, she said this because she knew I was Jewish. (But how?) I think she expected my disapproval. The truth is, I don't remember how I responded or what I felt. I did, however, thank her.

Gina

I WATCHED THE 2021 film, *My Tree*, by Jason Sherman, a Canadian filmmaker who went to Israel in search of the tree he was given at his Bar Mitzvah only to discover that it was planted on the remains of a Palestinian village destroyed in 1967. Since Israel was founded, the Jewish National Fund, JNF, started the tree planting program that became so well known to Americans. It seemed to offer a special opportunity for Jews to connect to the land of Israel and to the Jewish holiday, Tu BiShvat, the New Year of Trees.

But since its founding in 1901, JNF's initial focus was to displace Palestinian peasant farmers with Jewish settlers. Later, JNF bulldozers coordinated with Zionist militia to demolish Palestinian villages after expulsion, to erase their past. Palestinian land was turned into settlements for Jewish Israelis and destroyed villages were turned into "national parks" planted with pine trees, trees that are totally inappropriate for the region but familiar to Americans and Europeans.

Bragging about having planted 250 million trees, the JNF continues to deceive the world on its website today: From Barren Land to Afforestation: The Jewish National Fund's Tree Planting Efforts. Meanwhile, approximately two million olive trees that Palestinian growers depend upon for their livelihood have been destroyed by Israel and Israeli settlers in the last 75 years. The reason is exactly the same as the JNF: They are trying to destroy Palestinians' deepest connections to their land. The JNF, which holds almost half the seats on the governmental body that allocates most of Israel's land, has explicitly affirmed Jewish supremacy: its obligations are "to the Jewish people" and it does not work "for the benefit of all citizens of the state."

In 2022, I worked with local climate activists to plant mini-Forests in Brookline to mitigate the effects of climate change. Japanese botanist, Akira Miyawaki, proposed the planting of densely planted native trees in urban areas in 1976. These small forests cool and filter the air, store carbon, increase biodiversity, reduce flooding and erosion, and grow quickly. A local member of our team helped us celebrate plans for our first mini-Forest at her synagogue's celebration of Tu BiShvat. I asked whether she knew that American buyers of trees for Israel had been deceived about their purpose and had instead enabled settlement building for more than a century. She was surprised.

Israeli environmentalist Jay Shofet, who grew up in Connecticut, opposed planting trees in a Times of Israel blog: *This Tu BiShvat, don't plant a tree in Israel* (2020). Shofet's concern is not, however, the JNF's deception about why it plants trees. Instead, he simply reproduces the deception by proposing grasses which belonged in the ecosystem ages ago. Then he proposes re-branding Tu BiShvat from the New Year of Trees to the New Year for Animals. Jewish texts are the sources, he says, that inform ethical relationships with domesticated animals, especially now in light of industrial meat. I worry about industrial meat too. But Shofet's rebranding is again reproducing the cultural deception with animals rather than grasses: "We share this planet with other living creatures—animals wild and domesticated—and we must, for heaven's sake, and ours and theirs—do a much better job of looking out for them and their well-being." What about the Jewish texts that extend well being to neighbors and strangers that are human? Could Shofet not afford the same respect to the people who cared for the land for centuries before the Zionists arrived as he would to wild animals?

David

ONCE WHEN WE WERE taking a walk in our neighborhood, Gina said to me, "Israel is driving me crazy." She may also have said, "Jews are driving me crazy." Her antipathy to Zionism and its American supporters had become an obsession. And this was before October 7, 2023.

There were many flare-ups, even though by then we mostly agreed on the basics: Israeli apartheid was the root of the problem. Palestinians deserved freedom and equality. Gaza was the largest open-air prison in the world. The pro-Israel lobby had weaponized antisemitism. Still, her tirades, which I heard almost daily, her single-mindedness and her righteous indignation, were hard to bear. No matter how terribly Israel was treating the Palestinians, and how disgusted I was by its cruelty, I was unable simply to hate it.

I've spent a good chunk of my life thinking about Plato's *Republic,* and I've always been struck by what he says about democracy. On the one hand, he thinks it's a terrible form of government for it empowers citizens who are ignorant and self-interested to make decisions. It is inefficient, unstable and regularly succumbs to the lure of demagogues who convince the people that they have all the answers when in reality they are blowhards who care only about winning the next election. And yet, because a democracy allows citizens a significant measure of freedom, they are given the opportunity to carve out a private space of their own where they can do what they want. For this reason, a democracy can become an intensely interesting, vital, creative place, filled with different kinds of human beings doing and making different kinds of things. In short, it is double-edged, the best of the worst.

I mention this because it helps me articulate what I feel about being a citizen of the United States. During my lifetime, my country has done terrible things. It has fought devastating and pointless wars in Vietnam, Iraq and Afghanistan, and the military-industrial complex has attained an unspeakable level of power. It has helped destroy democratic movements in Latin America, Iran and Africa. Its massive consumer culture has contributed mightily to the pollution of the oceans and the warming of the atmosphere. Our public sphere has been hollowed out, the common good has been replaced by individual screens.

And yet, however cruel and sometimes hopeless the United States can often be, there is still room here for people—some, at least—to decide for themselves how they want to live. And this makes it, at times, beautiful.

Following Plato's lead, I have come to believe that the double-edge may be the best we can hope for when it comes to politics. And so when I look at Israel I cannot help but see it twice. Yes, without doubt it is an oppressive, cold-hearted killer. But that's not all it is, and not every Israeli citizen, or every Jew, embraces what it is doing. Which is why when Gina condemns Israel, full stop, and won't tolerate a word of qualification, I stiffen.

Gina

FACING HISTORY AND OURSELVES is a nonprofit that was founded in Brookline by two Massachusetts teachers in 1976. They wanted to provide resources to teachers, primarily for teaching about the history of the Holocaust, but also the Vietnam War and the civil rights' struggle. Since then Facing History has become a global entity, working in over 134 countries with an annual budget of over $50 million and reaching more than seven million students. A realtor had even mentioned it to me when we were planning to move to Brookline. Not long after moving here two teachers who were friends, and Jewish, told me how good Facing History resources were for teachers.

Over the years, however, I had been increasingly hearing criticism of their programs so I looked closely at their website offerings. I saw the overwhelming majority of classroom lessons were about the Holocaust (1623) and the second highest volume leapt across decades directly to the civil rights movement of the 60s (1392). I would not doubt the indispensable value of teaching these two subjects to our school children. But there were such gaps. I typed Nakba into the search bar and there were no resources (and there still are none). I typed "antisemitism" and found 329 resources. I typed "ethnic cleansing" and I found 197 entries such as the Rohingya, northern Ireland, the Nuremberg trials, the Holocaust, the Armenian Genocide, Darfur, Nanjing, American racism, and Kimchee on the Seder Plate—but nothing about Israel's ethnic cleansing.

I also found that Facing History had a Board of Scholars, a very impressive list of more than 60 people including Kwame Anthony Appiah, James Carroll, Henry Louis Gates Jr., and many professors of philosophy, international studies, psychology, ethics. Didn't they have questions about the gaps? So I wrote to many of them in the summer of 2019, invited them to talk and asked: If we are Facing History and Ourselves don't we and our students need to know not only about the refugees who fled the Holocaust but also the refugees created by the Israeli state that we hoped would solve the problems of Jewish refugees? None responded.

In January 2022, I attended a course from Facing History titled "Brave Classrooms: Taking on Antisemitism in Schools" that was designed for teachers. I took the course with two Jewish colleagues, one a child of Holocaust refugees and one whose husband is Palestinian. We joined the course with hope. We were encouraged by Facing History's stated values: "We stand up. We create space for each other. We act with empathy and kindness. We listen first and listen actively." But we were also skeptical since we knew they were supported by Israel lobbies such as the ADL. Would they bring forward a fear-based narrative that blinds Jews and others to everything but Jews' desire to feel safe and justifies all actions they take in pursuit of their own safety? Or would they take a broader anti-racist approach, understanding the unique and important specificities of contemporary antisemitism, including its weaponization against Palestinians and their allied social justice advocates?

We listened to lectures and participated in discussions on Zoom. The course explored Jew-hatred grounded in Christianity and traced it through the Middle Ages to the present. Focusing on a long, unbroken history of antisemitism gave the impression that hatred of Jews has been everywhere in the world since the beginning of time. There was no mention of how this hatred has been leveraged today for political and economic advantage. There were no references to how other religious or ethnic minorities have been treated, thus implying that antisemitism is inexplicably different from and worse than other forms of hatred.

Students in the course, teachers themselves, approached the course with earnest openness, answering questions given to them in the online discussion, a framework that discouraged students from asking their own questions. One of my colleagues used the discussion forum to comment that at no point in the four weeks had Facing History defined "antisemitism." When she pointed out that the IHRA redefinition of antisemitism included criticism of Israel and was often weaponized against Palestinians and their allies, Facing History's reaction was swift and decisive: They deleted her comments. I asked in the online discussion why the course had not talked about what had happened to Palestinians after the Holocaust. My comments were promptly deleted. Later a course facilitator explained that comments had been deleted because the course was not about "the geopolitical conflict." It was clear that Facing History was not, as they had stated, "actively listening." Can you imagine educators erasing comments written by teachers rather than having a discussion? Clearly this was not a "brave classroom." We were silenced. When will we be allowed to talk about what happened after the Holocaust? When will we be able to talk about anti-Muslim racism?

I had read Peter Beinart's essays in *New York Times* before I subscribed to The Beinart Notebook in 2022. I knew he had been the Editor of *The New Republic*. Beinart represents that rare combination where seriously studying and practicing Judaism led to developing relationships, even online, with Palestinians. Since David and I had retired during the pandemic we found ourselves having lunch together for the first time. He joined me on Fridays to listen to Beinart's interviews with a wide range of Jews, Palestinians, and others. Those conversations became part of our conversation. I admire Beinart's openness to conversations and his curiosity for different views. (In 2025 he published *Being Jewish After the Destruction of Gaza*.)

David

ALTHOUGH I DIDN'T RECOGNIZE it at the time, a pivotal moment came in July 2020. Gina had listened to a podcast in which the journalist Peter Beinart, about whom I knew nothing except his name, debated a couple of *New York Times* columnists on the question of Israel-Palestine. She described Beinart as making a case for a unified binational state in which Palestinians and Jews had equal rights, and suggested I listen to it too. I agreed, but in truth I didn't want to since I was getting tired of Gina's single-minded focus on Israel. Plus, the idea sounded fantastical. No way, I thought, would Jews ever agree to Palestinians becoming their fellow-citizens, for they are hell-bent on there being a Jewish nation. But I said I would do it, and so one hot afternoon I told her I was going to take a walk—it was during the pandemic and there wasn't much else to do—and listen to Beinart. She said she'd be glad to listen to it again, and so, earbuds in, we set out together.

To my surprise I found Beinart compelling. He argued that only full citizenship in a single state could give the Palestinians what they had been fighting for and deserved: equality, dignity, freedom, self-determination. He was calm, rational, clear, knowledgeable, and he had a stunning rejoinder to his opponents' predictable objection that a unified binational state was unrealistic. His parents were immigrants from South Africa and he said that when he was a kid the idea that white supremacy would end and black people would vote in democratic elections was dismissed as an impossible dream. But that's exactly what happened in 1994 when Nelson Mandela was elected as president. Beinart's combination of a strong intellect, eyes wide open to the harsh reality on the ground, and optimism floored me. He convinced me that the only reasonable, and possible, solution was one state shared equally by two peoples. I could not share in his optimism, but I found his logic impeccable.

When we got home I was hot, sweaty and badly in need of a shower, but that didn't stop me from telling Gina how impressed I was. And grateful that she had pressured me into listening to the podcast.

Gina

WHEN ISRAEL WAS BOMBING Gaza back in 2014, both Democratic and Republican lawmakers, often with the help of Israel lobbies, introduced anti-boycott bills across the U.S. They were retaliating against the success of the global nonviolent movement BDS, organized in 2005 to Boycott, Divest, Sanction Israel until its obligations under international law were met. Lawmaker's bills were designed to shield Israel from accountability and to suppress Palestinian-rights activism. Many states, but not Massachusetts, passed anti-boycott laws. These bills opened the way for an assault on boycotts themselves, even though boycotts are a time-honored tool of political expression. In Boston, we still celebrate the 1768 boycott of imported goods that were unfairly taxed by the British.

Anti-boycott bills led to bills designed to change the meaning of antisemitism—to expand the definition to include speech critical of Israeli policies. The idea of doing so had been in the making for decades. In the 1960s Zionist organizations in the U.S. and elements of the Israeli government saw anticolonial liberation movements across the globe as a threat. In 1974 the ADL published *The New Anti-Semitism*, aimed at defending Israel. In the 2000s, grassroots organizing around BDS and Palestinian solidarity revived Israeli fears. First published in 2005, the International Holocaust Remembrance Alliance's (IHRA-WDA) working definition of antisemitism was non-legally binding, intended for data collection and not for policy or legislation, according to its lead author Kenneth Stern. Heavily criticized by scholars and free speech advocates, nevertheless, IHRA officially adopted the definition in 2016.

Since then Zionist-supported legal teams have packaged the redefinition of antisemitism for inclusion in bills in towns and states across the country, and globally. Seven out of eleven examples of antisemitism in the IHRA definition focus on criticism of Israel such as denying the Jewish people their right to self-determination, claiming the State of Israel is a racist endeavor, accusing

Israel of exaggerating the Holocaust and drawing comparisons between contemporary Israeli society and that of the Nazis. With thousands of bills to read, many elected officials who voted for them thought they were doing the right thing to oppose antisemitism without realizing the bills were designed not to protect Jews but to protect Israel.

Antony Lerman's book *Whatever Happened to Antisemitism? Redefinition and the Myth of the 'Collective Jew,'* 2020, explains how Israel and its advocates redefined antisemitism to silence legitimate political speech that criticizes Israeli policies. What does it mean for me? That I cannot say Israeli policies support Jewish supremacy in Israel or occupied Palestine? That I cannot say that Israel has weaponized the Holocaust to support its military endeavors? The IHRA definition of antisemitism accuses even those practicing Judaism, as well as "cultural Jews" who criticize Israel, of being antisemitic. How ironic is that for the Jewish State? Most of all, it has confused the protection of Jews with the protection of Israel.

David

ANOTHER LANDMARK: AT SOME point in 2022, I joined Gina in watching The Beinart Notebook, a weekly Zoom "show," in which he discusses Israel-Palestine with his guests. I did so at her urging and largely in the hope of fortifying our relationship. I had no idea how significantly it would shape my thinking.

Some background on Peter Beinart. He is a long time journalist who began his career at *The New Republic* in 1995. He became its editor in 1999, a position he held for seven years. In 2003 he strongly supported the invasion of Iraq, yet another American war that proved to be disastrous. To his great credit, Beinart acknowledged his mistake when he learned that this war was justified on the basis of a lie: that Saddam Hussein possessed weapons of mass destruction.

An even more impressive turn on his part is that Beinart, an observant Jew and once a staunch Zionist, has become a radical critic of both Israel and its American enablers. Like Gina, he is now willing to call the 1948 war by the Arabic word Palestinians use: the Nakba, which means "catastrophe." Beinart's thinking changed for one simple reason: he listened to Palestinians. He read books by authors such as Ali Abunimah, Mahmoud Darwish and Edward Said, and came to see things, not just from his own Jewish perspective, but through Palestinian eyes. He learned much about what Israel actually did to the Palestinians in 1948, and about the conditions in which they have been forced to live since then in Gaza and the West Bank. He came to understand that, first and foremost, Palestinians are a people who have been uprooted and deprived of their rights.

Peter Beinart's evolution from Zionist to critic of Israel must have been painful. His paternal grandparents fled Lithuania before World War II and moved to South Africa, and he is a studious Jew who loves going to synagogue. Nonetheless, he forced himself to seek the truth about the history and present day reality of Palestine, and not simply to view Israel through the lens of Jewish suffering.

The Beinart Notebook invites its audience to do the same. By watching his show with Gina, I have "met" dozens of Palestinian journalists, scholars, artists and activists, who have, calmly and rationally, taught me a lot about how thoroughly the Zionist story has concealed the truth. I have also learned from Jewish scholars that Zionism was not always the monolithic and murderous force it is now. In the first decades of its existence there was much debate among Jews about what their homeland should be, and the notion of a binational state was taken seriously. Finally, however, one conception prevailed—a Jewish nation at all costs—and it required the expulsion of the Palestinians and the mobilization of support of diaspora Jews. Opposition to this version of Zionism was so thoroughly quashed that today almost any criticism is Israel is automatically condemned as antisemitic.

As the months passed, watching the Beinart show with Gina over lunch became a ritual. It's on Fridays, and I came to think of it as my own version of Shabbat.

Gina

REPORTERS AT THE *BOSTON Globe,* and most corporate newspapers, frequently equate anti-Zionism with being anti-Israel or antisemitic based on confusion from the IHRA redefinition. This conflation is irresponsible. If the meaning of Zionism is not clear—ethnonationalism—Jews, Israelis and others who are critical of Israel will be cast as antisemites. There are plenty of anti-Zionist organizations in Israel and the U.S. and there are plenty of Jews around the world who oppose Israel's ethnic cleansing. Criticism of Israeli policies is not anti-Jewish hate.

But these labels are complicated; after all, Israel calls itself the Jewish State. But all Israelis are not Jewish though Jewish Israelis benefit from their national status. There are also Palestinian Israelis, Christian Israelis, and Arab Jews who often describe themselves as ethnically Arab. But, most importantly, far more Zionists live in the U.S. than in Israel. Most of them are not Jewish. (Think Mike Huckabee, Trump's 2024 Ambassador to Israel). The largest Zionist group in the U.S. is Christians United for Israel (CUFI) mobilized by Pastor John Hagee who has a long history of stoking antisemitism. (Nevertheless, Christian Zionists in the US are eagerly supported by Israeli and some Jewish organizations. Still, it was quite shocking to see Senator Chuck Schumer join Hagee, who spoke at the largest pro-Israel rally in U.S. history in November, 2023, led by the Jewish Federation and the Council of Presidents of Major American Jewish Organizations.) Just as being critical of Israel doesn't automatically make someone antisemitic, being pro-Israel doesn't necessarily make them an ally either.

A conversation with a friend from graduate school helped me to understand how this confusion curses ordinary conversation, making it difficult to talk about Israel and Jews. Since she lives several states away, we keep in touch by long phone calls every month or so. Neither of us is Jewish but both of our husbands are. For my birthday, she had sent me a Jewish cookbook. In our next call, I was telling her about work I was doing to oppose Biden's support of weapons for Israel. This led her to apologize for sending me the cookbook. When I said I liked the book and it had no connection to Israeli policies, she said that she had messed up again. Distinguishing between Zionism and Jewish culture does not come naturally or easily. Silence is one product of this confusion.

In 2022, I heard about We Are Not Numbers, WANN, so named because the media so often reports on Palestinians only in terms of numbers—how many killed, injured, displaced. WANN introduces English writers to Gazans writing in English as a second or third language. WANN then publishes these stories about life under occupation and in refugee camps, on their website (and *We Are Not Numbers: The Voices of Gaza's Youth* by Ahmed Alnaouq & Pam Bailey, 2025). In my years as a mentor I have been introduced to more than a dozen young Palestinians, writing on their cellphones during frequent power outages, who share their stories about their families and neighbors: a family's Palestinian Museum that was destroyed, the targeted murder of a journalist uncle, multiple displacements, sleepless nights with a cellphone, death, living with the constant sound of drones and frequent bombings, and a farewell to childhood. (The Gaza office of WANN was invaded and partially destroyed by the IDF late in 2024.)

Ta-Nehisi Coates took his first trip to the occupied West Bank and Jerusalem in the summer of 2023, following visits to Dakar, Senegal, and Chapin, South Carolina. He chronicled his travels in *The Message* (2024). Coates understood the history and experience of what he calls "Western racecraft" so well that he could not only see its history but see it at work in Israel-Palestine. He describes WWII as a race war. The Nazis had looked to American race laws as models for their antisemitic laws in the 1930s. They considered Ukrainians and Poles, and all of Africa as "black." But "in the immediate post-war years, the place of Jews in the tent of whiteness was uncertain."

Coates describes the politicization of Jews into whiteness when citing journalist Kenneth Bilby's comments in 1951: "Israeli Jews were becoming physically separate from their Semitic cousin the Arab world." Bilby's explanation came after a visit to a kibbutz that year when he concluded that he couldn't tell Jewish children from British, American, German or Scandinavian children!

Coates' observations from his trip to the occupied territories—after he'd been questioned at many check-points and spoken with many Palestinians—brought the issue of race to the present: "I don't think I ever, in my life, felt the glare of racism burn stranger and more intense than in Israel." This was before October 7.

David

MY MEMORIES OF THE morning of October 7 are fuzzy. At first it seemed like more of the horrible, predictable same: a Hamas attack sure to be followed by an Israeli bombing of Gaza. I don't know when the magnitude became clear. Hours later? Days? But when the stark reality did sink in, I felt nothing but dread. The response, I feared, would be massive and merciless. I thought about one of the few biblical stories, from the Book of Samuel, that I've read, and that I know some Israeli leaders today continue to invoke. The Lord commands Saul, the first king of Israel, to attack the Amalekites. They are a tribe who, in the Book of Exodus, are said to have attacked the Israelites as they were fleeing from Egypt. Not only is Saul told to kill their soldiers but, in order to exact proper vengeance, to put to death all their men, women, children, infants, cattle, sheep, camels and donkeys; in other words, to commit genocide. Saul does kill all the people but he spares their king, Agag, and the animals that could be eaten, perhaps because his own men were hungry. For his disobedience the Lord forsakes him and he is doomed.

I imagine rabbis and scholars have interpreted this story in many different and complicated ways. Still, the simple question remains: what kind of God would do such a thing? And what kind of people would follow His orders?

On October 10 Peter Beinart sent a video to his subscribers, *Blessed Are You God, Who Sets Captives Free*, and for ten minutes spoke to us of his anguish. Over a thousand Israelis—men, women, children and infants—were murdered. And he spoke of his struggle. How could he express his deep love of the Jewish people without resorting to the same failed strategy for keeping Jews safe that Israel has been pursuing for seventy-five years: hammering the Palestinians harder, killing more of them, oppressing them even more relentlessly. He was passionate, and deeply logical, in his reminder that if this policy were effective, October 7 would not have happened, and that even if Hamas were to be completely annihilated other Palestinians would take up the fight for freedom and dignity.

He ended what I think of as his sermon by putting a yarmulke on his head and reciting a prayer that observant Jews, like him, read every morning: "Blessed are you God, who sets captives free." Unlike too many Jews who prayed that day, he had both Israelis and Palestinians in mind. I was so moved, and convinced, that I sent the link to those of my friends I thought would watch it.

Gina

ON THURSDAY AFTER OCTOBER 7, I was so upset by the violence in Israel-Palestine, the war crimes committed by Hamas's military and the fear of Israeli revenge, that I felt I had to personally do something. I went to my local farmers market as I do each week but, instead of buying produce, I stood on the sidewalk and handed out copies of an Op-Ed from the *Boston Globe* by Abdallah Fayyad: "The Cycle of Violence Starts with the Israeli Occupation." I had a few good conversations, faced some indifference, was yelled at, aggressively photographed with cell phones, and even snubbed by a couple of friends. Who was it among these strangers and friends who thought the occupation was ok with them and didn't think it was the root cause of the conflict? Did they not know about the occupation or that it was illegal? That the people whose families had lived there for generations could no longer move about freely? That their land was under Israeli control and they were not able to vote for the people who would make decisions about it? This was the first time in my life that I have taken a stand by myself on a public sidewalk. I feared the worst to come.

Later in October, our Boston chapter of JVP met in a Baptist Church with a tall steeple and a large rainbow flag in Jamaica Plain. Our chapter was now flooded with new members, mostly young people who were joining the older generation who had been building the chapter for years. The minister introduced herself, welcomed us and thanked us for our work without even mentioning hers. I found out later that she had taken many groups from New England to the West Bank to see what occupation looks like.

Following speeches, small group discussions and dinner, we were cleaning up when I asked a JVP friend: Why don't we ever meet in a synagogue? Her near laughter totally surprised me. Didn't I know, she said, that synagogues require large capital investments that are funded largely by conservatives who support Israel? I didn't. But I probably should have known that since Reform Jewish congregations who are progressive often operate on a shoestring. I'd been to a local Jewish Workers' Circle event that was located in a borrowed space off an alley on Harvard Street and, in Iowa, a church shared its space with the Reform Congregation.

I remember watching a short video after the massacre of Gaza began that made a lasting impression on me. In it, three comedians asked: "Who is Hamas? Old people? They're Hamas. Women? Definitely Hamas. Babies? Hamas." Israel duplicitously claimed its bombing of civilians in Gaza was military defense when in reality it was ethnic cleansing. Hamas is an authoritarian Sunni government, elected in 2006, that provides social services to 2.3 million refugees trapped in Gaza. An armed wing of Hamas of about 40,000 fighters, Al-Qassam Brigades, are the ones, along with some escapees, who violently attacked Israel on October 7.

A close friend of mine asked me, months into the destruction of Gaza, how else could Israel fight Hamas if they're hiding among the general population? Well, the Geneva Conventions were agreed to by Israel and the United States after the horrors of World War II to establish standards meant to protect civilian populations even from militants who might be hiding. They were intended to prevent warring nations from engaging in barbaric actions that include bombing civilians while using the defense of having "intelligence" that a terrorist was hidden among them. But it was the comedy skit more than international law that clarified for me why Israel's response was so genocidal, long before the word was commonly used.

On October 12, the *Brookline News* reported that "The Brookline Superintendent apologizes after email on Israel that 'fell short.'" How did he fall short? The Superintendent was reprimanded for writing an email to the community on the School website about the pain we were all suffering from escalating violence in Israel. Consequently he was pressured by some Jews, Israelis, Town Meeting members, and our State Representative Vitolo to apologize for not toeing the Zionist line. As he was told to do, he condemned Hamas's attack and exceptionalized Israeli suffering.

In a letter published days later, I could only thank the Superintendent for his initial response to everyone's grief.

On October 15, our Tree Team from Mothers Out Front, and the Town officials that we had been working with, planted our first Miyawaki mini-Forest in a small local gesture to mitigate the effects of climate change. It was a gorgeous fall day and people were so eager to contribute locally to something that might ease impending climate disasters that one hundred volunteers planted more than 500 small trees and shrubs in three hours. Retirees, children, and every age between, dug in. A filmmaker captured it. It was a joyous day for local action that briefly took my mind off international news.

Two days later David and I left for a little vacation in Santa Barbara. Our older daughter joined us and it was impossible to avoid talking about the violence in Gaza and Israel. The Jewish Federation had banners up and down the pedestrian street at the center of town which made me feel like the Israel lobby was already digging in to silence dissent. All three of us, for the first time, felt it might help us to attend a protest, even on vacation. It was held at a heavily trafficked intersection. The organizers supplied us with ceasefire signs. The experience was unsatisfying. It didn't feel in any way like we'd contributed to the conversation our country needed to have about a ceasefire but it mattered to me that our family was not simply silent about what our country was doing.

David

GINA AND I USUALLY do our travelling through Home Exchange, a platform that connects people who want to swap homes. A family from Santa Barbara, California approached us. They wanted to spend a week in Boston, October 17–26, 2023. It had never occurred to us to visit Santa Barbara but we thought, why not? The pictures of their house looked great, it was close to the beach and, except for airfare, it would be free. What sealed the deal for us was that our older daughter, who lives in Portland, Oregon, said she'd be able to join us for a few days.

Our vacation began ten days after Hamas attacked Israel. I can't remember how lethal the Israeli bombardment was at that point, but even then I was sure a bloodbath was coming. If nothing else, Israel is predictable. If Palestinians kill a single Jew, they kill a hundred in return. For years the IDF had been "mowing the lawn" in Gaza. This seemingly innocuous phrase refers to the Israeli strategy of retaliating to Hamas' missiles with periodic bombings, in which not only fighters but innocent women and children are killed and homes, schools and hospitals are destroyed. Disproportionate response, it's called, and even if it is done to deter further attacks it violates a cardinal principle of classical just war theory. "Mowing the lawn" is a chilling metaphor that makes killing human beings seem to be entirely normal.

The very evening we arrived in Santa Barbara, Gina did some online hunting and, sure enough, she discovered through the JVP website that a demonstration would take place not far from us in a couple of days. The three of us went. It was held in downtown Santa Barbara on the sidewalks of a busy intersection. The protestors, several of whom were Palestinian students from the local university, were holding signs and chanting at the cars flying by, some of which responded by beeping their horns. Whether in solidarity or anger was impossible to tell. Gina was in her element but, even though I was willing to be identified with the demonstrators, I didn't like the feeling of being sucked into a crowd bellowing its opinions to strangers. A strangely wooden sort of middle-aged man approached me and began to pepper me with questions. He was calm and non-confrontational, and so at first I thought he was actually trying to have a reasonable conversation, but this quickly gave way to the realization that he was a blockhead with no interest in anything other than his own opinions (which, as far as I could figure out, were hostile). I stalked away from him.

The remainder of our vacation was a peculiar blend of gloom, fury, and long walks on the beautiful beach or in the hills. Gina was preoccupied and radiated hostility. She began every morning in Santa Barbara with a harsh, blunt tirade. Her main target was usually the President of the United States, Joe Biden, who from the outset had pledged unconditional support of Israel and given it billions of dollars of military aid, which it then spent buying weapons from American manufacturers. Sometimes she seemed to be angry at me for not being more like her—enraged at her country and determined to do something about it—but I couldn't be sure. Her aggressive moral certainty put me on edge. I don't like the feeling of being bullied.

While Gina was glued to her computer screen, I spent hours in our backyard, basking in Southern California sunshine, and reading Larry McMurtry's *Lonesome Dove*. Among its other virtues, this marvelous book lays bare the brutality at the heart of the 19th-century American West. It spoke well, I thought, to the moment.

Gina

IN NOVEMBER, I JOINED hundreds of protesters in a coalition of groups organized by Massachusetts Peace Action. Vice President Kamala Harris was attending a private fundraiser at the Ritz Carlton Hotel next to the Boston Commons for the Democratic National Committee. Inside the hotel, Harris was reported to have affirmed to the DNC that she and the President supported Israel's right to defend itself and that civilians shouldn't be intentionally targeted. Could they not have known of the violence they were enabling? Or were they simply politicians saying what they thought would get them re-elected?

The primary message of demonstrators was support for a ceasefire, which two thirds of Americans supported at the time, and to protest the Biden administration's military aid to Israel. The police presence was very visible but not aggressive. I stood at the edge of the Commons holding one end of a very long CEASEFIRE banner, as long as my arms could hold it. Many posters said The People Charge Genocide before the word was commonly used. Chants at that protest were the most aggressive I had heard, such as: Israel bombs, USA pays, how many kids did you kill today? While not untrue, the chants chilled me. The protest didn't feel very satisfying. Obviously Harris was not moved.

I felt much more satisfied by the FREE PALESTINE pin that I wear everyday and the bumper sticker on my front porch than the protests I had attended. It would seem that a really large rally would be valuable for solidarity if not changing minds. But I hadn't felt connected to the people at most rallies. I didn't like being told what to say in call-and-response chants. Rallies need music, especially live music, for growing gatherings of people together for the pleasure of solidarity, more like the ones I remember from the Vietnam protest days, dancing and picnicking rather than yelling.

One of my neighbors and a member of JVP was so desperate to respond to the assault on Gaza that she resolved to act on her own. During the summer and fall of 2024 she spent some time nearly everyday camped out at Coolidge Corner, the subway stop and commercial center of Brookline, with a comfortable chair and a sign that said, "Another Jewish mother against the slaughter of Palestinian children." I could not do what she was doing without my blood pressure skyrocketing but I would often talk with her there, among supporters and detractors who dropped by. Once I got into a conversation with an Israeli family that was visiting Boston. They seemed to be trying to defend Israel when they told us that a large number, maybe a majority, of physicians in Israel were Palestinian. But what it told me was that Israelis should have grave doubts about the future of their own healthcare when they were ethnically cleansing their physicians' relatives.

Another time I talked with an Israeli student who attended the Berklee College of Music who said his parents had owned the Soda Stream company and he was so earnestly telling me, without explanation, that Americans just didn't understand Israel. One other time I was holding one end of a Free Palestine banner when a young girl pointed to our sign to get her family's attention. Then her mother told us they were Palestinian and thanked us.

In July, my JVP neighbor took a bus to D.C. to join the opposition to unconditional military aid to Israel in the rotunda of the Cannon Congressional Office Building. Although the gathering was largely to protest Biden's compliance in giving arms to Israel, it was also the day before Netanyahu had been invited to speak by both parties of Congress. With protesters waving banners saying No One is Free Until Everyone is Free and wearing red shirts that said Jews Say Stop Arming Israel and Not in My Name on the back, she was arrested for the first time in her life at age 79. She told me that she was not physically roughed up but her hands were bound with zip ties and she was made to wait 9 hours before being released.

Months into Israel's war on Gaza, I ordered STOP ARMING ISRAEL buttons to wear and I replaced the word APARTHEID with GENOCIDE ISN'T KOSHER on the rocking chair on our front porch. It's hard to say what these words meant to people. A young man just walking by is the only person who commented, saying he liked it because it led to a family conversation. Are people so afraid of talking about U.S. support for Israel, as I was, for fear of being accused of antisemitism? Some people in Brookline have yard signs with the Israeli flag that say We Stand with Israel. I wonder as I walked by their houses if they would say they support genocide. But I haven't talked with them.

On New Year's Eve after Oct 7 the weather was not bad for the middle of winter. So David and I walked a couple of miles to a JVP-initiated protest at the Federal Building near City Hall in downtown Boston where Senators Warren and Markey's offices were located. We walked through the crowd, greeted a few friends, noticed the Hasidic Satmars prominently poised with their strings, curls, and banners in support of a ceasefire. As soon as the call-and response began, we walked to an adjacent ice sculpture display and took the train home. For us it had been an occasion for walking, showing up, and seeing the festivities.

Following Israel's ongoing assault, increasing numbers of headlines in the *Boston Globe* claimed rising levels of antisemitism, headlines far more rampant than photos of rubble in Gaza. The headlines felt like an assault on readers in defense of enabling more violence. I wrote to the Editor of the *Boston Globe* in January questioning the lack of a definition of antisemitism in the paper's reporting. Consequently, the Editor invited a dozen people from our letter-to-editors group (largely JVP) to a working lunch at the paper's offices. The Editor clarified the distinction between News journalism and Editorial, which deferred to the Editorial Board, as well as the *Globe*'s dependence on the *New York Times* for national and international news. We made the argument that reporters had the responsibility, if they used the word "antisemitism," to inform readers whether it was based on a definition that included criticism of Israel. Our meeting was collegial but I haven't seen *Globe* or *New York Times*' reporters take responsibility for clarifying this definition in their reporting. Most also default to reporting data from the Anti-Defamation League, ADL, whose mission has become one of defending Israel from criticism. Even Wikipedia has identified the ADL as an unreliable source of reporting. (In July, 2025, the three million-membership of the National Education Association, the largest teachers' union in the U.S., approved a measure that the NEA "will not use, endorse, or publicize materials from the Anti-Defamation League, ADL.") Why can't corporate news organizations figure this out? Israel has blocked global news outlets from reporting from Gaza, the IDF has attacked media offices, and Israel has targeted and killed some American and hundreds of Palestinian journalists. Yet, corporate journalists have been largely silent.

The most thoughtful discussion that I have heard in Brookline on the subject of Israel-Palestine was presented by Brookline Booksmith and the Brookline Peace Coalition in March, 2024: Brookline for Peace in Palestine and Israel: Past, Present, and Where We Go From Here. It was the rarest of occasions: a panel of Jews and Palestinians, academics (including Omer Bartov), and activists, speaking together about Israel's war and U.S. support for it, in hope of envisioning a peaceful future. Hundreds of people attended and it felt like a local version of one of Beinart's conversations.

When our daughters were both visiting us in May, 2024, our family attended a Standout for Peace designed to encourage our Town Meeting members to vote for a ceasefire warrant article. The speakers were clergy, a Palestinian mother of Brookline students, and an Israeli surgeon who spoke intelligently and respectfully for a lasting ceasefire, safe return of hostages, and humanitarian aid. But it was difficult to hear because the Zionist crowd, waving Israeli flags, were using bullhorns to drown out our speakers. When a siren went off repeatedly creating alarm, David asked a police officer about it. He was told it was from their bullhorns. Debate was further silenced in our little town when Town Meeting members would twice vote to table ceasefire resolutions.

GINA

In June, 2024, an Op-Ed appeared in the newsletter of Brookline PAX, a local organization that claims to "promote world peace." Marty Rosenthal, Co-Chair of PAX, wrote the Op-Ed that, ironically, opposed a ceasefire resolution being considered by our Town Meeting. Not only does this Co-Chair of PAX oppose a ceasefire resolution, he plays every Zionist trope, from the "eight-millenia" history of the Jewish race and its victimhood right up to the Holocaust. The response I sent to all members of Brookline's Town Meeting:

> Rosenthal's tirade uses the politically-motivated IHRA working definition of antisemitism which accuses millions of Jews and non-Jews alike of being antisemitic because they have criticized Israeli policies while American Zionists, many of whom are white supremacist Christians, are encouraged to continue their unconditional support of Israel.

> Rosenthal's support isn't for Jews or Judaism; it is for Zionism. Young Jews from If Not Now and Jewish Voice for Peace, who don't identify their Judaism with Israel, are the ones who are saving Jews from the antisemitism Rosenthal fears. They see clearly that providing impunity to Israeli violence against civilians is not in the interest of Jews and Americans. Israeli safety does not depend on the destruction of the Palestinian people but on their liberation.

> Rosenthal speaks of the "eight-millenia" history of antisemitism and the Holocaust without saying a single word about the death, displacement, and suffering of Gazan civilians and the pogroms in the West Bank during the past seven months, nor about the murder and mass expulsions of Palestinians from their homes at the founding of Israel, nor the ethnic cleansing and apartheid against Palestinians during the 75 years of Israel's existence.

David

As the siege of Gaza intensified, its horror became undeniable.
Gina called it a "genocide," a term I resisted for a long time. "Ethnic
cleansing" seemed more accurate to me. But as the months passed
I began to waver. Hospitals and schools, power plants and water
infrastructure, were being methodically bombed. Israel was not
just killing tens of thousands of Palestinians, it was destroying everything needed to sustain life in Gaza.

During this awful stretch, I had to force myself to listen to
The Beinart Notebook, for it had become quite painful. To name
just a few of his Palestinian guests: Laila Al-Arian, the executive
producer of "The Night Won't End," which Beinart described as
"an extraordinarily powerful documentary about three families in
Gaza during this war;" Ghassan Abu-Sittah, Musallma Abu Khalil
and Lina Qassen-Hassan, three physicians who have worked in
Gaza; Rashid Khalidi, whom Beinart describes as "America's most
eminent historian of the Palestinian people and the Palestinian
struggle." Their stories were nearly unbearable. Whatever label it is
finally given, the destruction of Gaza is hell on earth.

Among the most powerful, and almost reassuring, of Beinart's discussions were ones with Israeli Jews who, despite facing
a torrent of denunciation from their fellow-citizens, are nonetheless vocal critics of their own country. Omer Bartov "is one of the
world's most prominent scholars of the Holocaust. He's also an Israeli who has warned about the genocidal rhetoric of some Israeli
leaders since October 7." Yael Sternhell, a Professor of History at
Tel Aviv University, is the daughter of a Holocaust survivor and
a long time peace activist. Gideon Levy is a journalist who, having spent the past thirty years exposing the violent oppression of
Palestinians in the West Bank, is now regularly accused of being a
traitor by his neighbors. But, like Beinart, he does not succumb to
despair. He goes forward. He persists.

Our sharing of The Beinart Notebook has brought us closer.
The words Nakba, "settler-colonialist," "ethnic cleansing" and

"genocide" are now part of my own vocabulary when I enter into discussions of Israel.

Gina

THE *BOSTON GLOBE* PUBLISHED an opinion piece in December, 2024, whose author, Joan Leegant, accused a bookstore and the New York Writers Festival of calling Jewish writers "Zionist" and using it as an epithet to exclude Jews from the publishing record. In a published letter, below, I accused both the *Globe* and the author of conflating all Jews and Israelis with Zionism. Israel's hateful violence and its live-streamed murder of civilians and destruction the past year is all the more reason to clearly distinguish Zionists from anti-Zionist Jews and Israelis. It is furthermore not enough to remain silent. The New York Writers Festival was clarifying the confusion by simply asking writers to say whether they support or oppose Zionism's genocide. The *Globe* later changed the title to "Zionism label casts a chill through the literary world."

> The *Globe* and author Joan Leegant need to choose their words more carefully. The Google survey, the assistant manager of the Chicago bookstore, and the New York Writers Festival all appropriately used the word Zionist for people who support Israel's injustices to Palestinians. But the *Globe*'s headline—"Jewish authors confront growing backlash in literary world"—and Leegant conflate opposition to Zionism as being "anti-Israel" or anti-Jewish. This boycott is not anti-Israel or anti-Jewish. There are plenty of anti-Zionist organizations in Israel that oppose Israel's prejudices against non-Jews, and there are plenty of Jews around the world who oppose Israel's hateful occupation. The boycott against Israeli cultural institutions is aimed at those who "are complicit in violating Palestinian rights, including . . . justifying Israel's occupation, apartheid, or genocide" and "have never publicly recognized the inalienable rights of the Palestinian people as enshrined in international law." Leegant raises concerns about the reception of her book but offers no position on Israel's policies, so a question remains: Is she a Zionist?

The question goes beyond whether Leegant is a Zionist. Not only writers but also politicians and organizations can no longer remain silent. Each needs to understand what Zionism means—Israeli ethnonationalism—and clarify whether they are Zionists or anti-Zionists because there is no middle ground in genocide.

In 2024 I attended a second course on antisemitism because its focus was A Curriculum on Antisemitism from a Framework of Collective Liberation, administered by PARCEO—a community research, resource, and education center focused on collective work for justice. I hoped that the idea of collective liberation suggested that while antisemitism was, like other hatreds, based on particular circumstances, hope for its elimination was tied to the hope of eliminating all others. The course tackled what antisemitism is and is not but I did not learn about the history of the term "antisemitism." It successfully avoided presenting the eternal narrative of antisemitism and it acknowledged its weaponization. Nevertheless I left thinking that any course that took as its subject "antisemitism," rather than a particular geographic or historical context, was still seeing antisemitism as exceptional. The Holocaust is exceptional hatred. Antisemitism is not.

PARCEO's course was nevertheless quite an improvement to the course on antisemitism I had taken from Facing History and Ourselves two years earlier. *Jewish Currents* reported in February 2025 that after Israel's assault on Gaza intensified in 2023 "more than 80 Facing History employees—around half of the nonprofit's US-based staff—sent a letter to the organization's leadership team criticizing what they said was a pro-Israel bias in educational materials, and a shirking of responsibility to 'address the risk of genocide against Palestinians.'" More than a year later some of its signatories said that Facing History had not only failed to revise their course, they had doubled down on their unwillingness to criticize Israel and their silence about the Nakba and the destruction of Gaza.

I've been asking a provocative question for decades: Why do Jews who aren't religious cling to Jewishness? I get it. It's ethnic. I don't have any problem with Jewish ethnicity. The problem I have is with accusations of antisemitism based on criticism of Zionism. Antisemitism is supposedly anti-Jewish hatred. I've been accused of antisemitism. But I've never felt hatred towards Jews. Why is antisemitism such a confusing term?

I knew that since the Middle Ages Christian leaders used their religion to murder, enslave, imprison and steal from Jews, pagans, Muslims, Christian heretics, and Romanies. What I hadn't known before reading Sim Kern's book, *Genocide Bad* (2025), was that "Antisemitism" was a Christian invention popularized by a German political party that was a forerunner of the Nazis. Kern uses the capital-A in Antisemitism to differentiate this nineteenth-century German invention from common usage today.

Why would Antisemites themselves have concocted the term "Antisemitism"? The word "Semitic" in the eighteenth century had described a group of languages, including Arabic and Hebrew, thought to be spoken by the descendents of biblical figures. But the people speaking those languages, termed "Semites," was narrowed to refer only to Jews in the 1860s when the secular German journalist Wilhelm Marr used the word "*Semitismus*" interchangeably with the word "*Judentum.*"

At the same time, Marr popularized the term that would replace the German word *Judenhass*, commonly used to mean the hatred of Jews, with the word, *Antisemitismus*, a word that would in 1881 be translated into English dictionaries as "anti-Semitism." What was going on in Germany at the time to account for this new term defining the hatred of Jews? In 1871, Jews were legally emancipated in the new Second German Empire and given rights equal to those of their Christian neighbors. Just eight years later, in 1879, Wilhelm Marr established the League of Antisemites, whose stated goal was reversing Jewish emancipation.

In "Towards a History of the Term Antisemitism," historian David Feldman explains that in the early twentieth century, the distinction that formed the meaning of this unfamiliar term, "Antisemitism," was racially based. Early German Antisemites believed that Jews were a different race and therefore no matter whether they were secular or tried to assimilate, they would remain a different race and a threat to the German nation. This racial definition of Antisemitism felt so novel that Jewish writers such as journalist Lucien Wolf were careful to distinguish this new Antisemitism taking hold in Germany from the older religious persecution, *Judenhass,* of Russia.

Zionists came to share key ideas with these early German Antisemites—that Jews are a distinct race and anyone who belongs to the Jewish race will never be at home in a non-Jewish nation. I had long known that Zionists collaborated with Balfour and other British antisemites to colonize Palestine. Wolf became an early anti-Zionist because he was critical of Zionists who agreed with Antisemites. Since Antisemitism expressed the erroneous view that Jews were members of a distinct race whose interests were separate from those of their fellow citizens, Wolf feared that claiming a nationality for themselves was likely to feed Jewish hatred.

We now know there is no scientific basis to race and that Jews in the U.S. have become equal U.S. citizens which makes the word "antisemitism" now seem anachronistic, a historical term representing pseudoscientific racism. But the same Antisemitism movement that began in Germany contributed to the policies of Jewish ethnic nationalism in the founding of Israel. Since then Israel's ethnonationalists have weaponized and lobbed "Antisemitism" around the world in defense of Zionism.

Noam Chomsky dates the "weaponization" of antisemitism to post-1967 when he quotes Israel's foreign minister Abba Eban saying in 1973: "One of the chief tasks of any dialogue with the Gentile world is to prove that the distinction between anti-Semitism and anti-Zionism is not a distinction at all. Anti-Zionism is merely the new anti-Semitism." He is clear: Antisemitism means disagreeing with Israel and there will be no debate about Zionism.

I didn't recognize this "weaponization" until 2023 when I joined JVP Boston's opposition to the attempt to codify the IHRA working definition of antisemitism into law in Massachusetts. It failed here twice but was adopted in many other states, the EU and many countries. Anti-Jewish hate can already be addressed under existing civil rights laws as religious, race or ethnic discrimination. Why would we need another term? IHRA redefines antisemitism, formerly anti-Jewish hatred, to include criticism of Israel, contradicting the historical collaboration between Antisemites and Zionism. About the time that the IHRA redefinition was proposed, the word "anti-Semitism," was recommended to be spelled without the hyphen and capital-S to further separate Jewish ethnicity from its broader Semitic heritage.

Since Hamas' violent attack on Israel on October 7, major newspapers have been weaponizing antisemitism with headlines on nearly a daily basis to distract attention away from the live-stream massacre Israel was committing. They reported antisemitism on campuses where students, many of whom were Jewish, were trying to communicate the seriousness of Israel's bombing of tens of thousands of civilians. Reporters regularly sensationalized a "pervasive" antisemitism while getting their data from the ADL, a self-described lobby for Israel. With its weaponization I have seen the power "antisemitism" has had to silence speech at our local public school, Town Meeting, the State legislature and the Special Commission for Combatting Antisemitism that was organized after Israel's vengeance against Gaza began. The protean history of the word "antisemitism," changing from collaboration with Antisemites to opposing antisemitism, explains the confusion and the suspicion the term provokes.

When I said to David, Israel is driving me crazy, it was the insanity of a barrage of "antisemitism" headlines about a few cases of potential anti-Jewish hate crimes by contrast to the paltry reporting on the massive death and destruction caused by our bombs in Israel's hands. This was incomprehensible. But not the end of it.

Now the Trump administration is exploiting the slippery term "antisemitism" to defend attacks on immigrants, higher education, free speech, public media, diversity, equity, and inclusion initiatives, and more. Surely this signals the end of the usefulness of this term and the need to deposit it into the historical dustbin of 1850–1970. I agree with those who are proposing we dispense with the term altogether. Sim Kern concludes Zionism is antisemitism.

Anti-Jewish hate is a better term, legal and emptied of politics, for a crime against Judaism or Jewish ethnicity, that must be protected, just like anti-Palestinian hate, anti-LGBTQ hate or any other hate crime.

David

I HAVE COME TO think differently about being Jewish; more spe-
cifically, about Jewish victimhood. Antisemitism, I am sure, has
long been a virulent force in Christian Europe. (If anyone has
doubts about this, I suggest reading James Carroll's *Constantine's
Sword: The Church and the Jews*.) My ancestors fled from Russia
because of it, and those relatives who failed to do so were killed by
it. Through years of cultural conditioning, this basic fact has been
stamped into my conception of myself. This is why after seeing
the film *Genocide* in 1982 with my Ramaz students, I blurted out,
"I have never felt so Jewish." Only now do I see how strange that
remark was. Does being a Jew mean to identify with the history of
Jewish suffering? How could this be when I myself have suffered so
little during my seventy-four years in America? What did it mean
for me to feel Jewish when I was not observant? I had been taught
by my parents that all human beings are, in the most important
sense, equal, and I've lived by this principle ever since. Why, then,
did I feel such a surge of identification when I saw images of ema-
ciated Jews and mounds of discarded shoes on the screen? What is
the attraction? What is the need?

The horror of Israel's destruction of Gaza has made me realize
a simple truth: victims are shaped by what they have suffered, and
sometimes their humanity is ruined in the process. Little wonder
when they become victimizers themselves.

A while back I read several novels by I. J. Singer (the brother
of the famous I. B. Singer). He was a historically minded, realis-
tic writer who depicted Jewish life in Eastern Europe in the late
nineteenth and early twentieth centuries. Singer's books depict not
only the relentless pressure of antisemitism, but also how it turned
some of its victims into monsters. He unsparingly shows us the
ugliness of megalomaniacal and misogynist Hasidic rabbis, ruth-
lessly ambitious and wealthy industrialists, and Jews who came to
despise their own Yiddish past. Singer taught me that it is possible
to admit there are Jews who, after having suffered terribly, have

inflicted terrible suffering on others—without being an antisemite. He, along with Gina and Peter Beinart, helped me realize it is possible to decry the power of the Zionist lobby in American politics without succumbing to the vile fantasies of the *Protocols of the Elders of Zion*.

Singer's heroes, if he had any, were Jews like my parents who believed that the solution to "the Jewish Question" could only be found in solidarity with all human beings.

I've come to think of those Jews who have engineered the destruction of Gaza as descendants of the twisted fierce characters who populate Singer's books. They have killed an unspeakable number of innocent people without an iota of compassion for anyone other than their fellow Jews, and sometimes not even for them.

A sad truth, perhaps, is lurking. Victims will victimize others, and one way or another human beings will always be at one another's throats. Jews are no exception.

The most recent landmark on the map of my past: in August of 2025 I read *One Day, Everyone Will Have Always Been Against This*, by Omar El Akkad. A memoir, replete with astute observations about politics, immigration, literature and liberalism, it is a searing book. El Akkad, a brilliant writer, has been driven nearly mad, not only by the slaughter of tens, perhaps hundreds, of thousands of Palestinians in Gaza, but by the active complicity, and mind boggling hypocrisy, of the United States. How is it possible, he asks, for human beings to witness the killing of so many utterly innocent children and not be moved? Now that the facts are in— the genocide has, after all, been livestreamed—how is it possible for so many Americans to remain silent?

El Akkad's book has helped me understand Gina better, for she has asked precisely this question for a long time, and she too has been driven nearly mad. I now better appreciate that her anguish has been an appropriate emotional response to the horrors we have not only witnessed, but also paid for with our tax dollars.

Gina

ISRAEL HAS GRAZED EVERY aspect of my life—my personal relationships, my town, state, and country—even my profession. What I did not know more than twenty-five years ago when I helped publish *Shlomo Aronson* was how Israeli politics governed landscape projects. It's not that I didn't know politics impact culture but I didn't know Israeli politics. My secular Jewish Israeli colleague's review of the book described its subtitle, "*Making Peace with the Land,*" as addressing conflicts over land that had altered it from its "abundant state described in biblical texts." Now I recognize the message: Ancient Israel had been a land of abundance that religious Jews believe biblical texts promised to them but which interlopers had destroyed in the centuries before they came back to repair it.

Archaeological parks have been well funded in Israel and several were presented in the book. One was Beit Guvrin-Maresha National Park, a 1250-acre park whose primary historical structures are underground—a network of 500 caves that were carved out of limestone since prehistory. Aronson was commissioned to create the infrastructure above ground—a visitors' center, parking, trails, and thousands of olive, fig, and other fruit trees—on a site that had never before seen tourists.

Biblical archaeology has been called a sport in Israel. The process often begins by displacing Palestinians to begin excavations for projects, such as national parks, and then erasing Arabic names and histories. Beit Guvrin-Maresha National Park is named for the remains of two historical towns in the Park. Maresha is the Hebrew name given to the remains of a city mentioned in the Book of Joshua that were excavated from the Arabic town of Tell Sandahannah. Beit Guvrin, is the Hebrew name that replaced Beit Jibrin, an Arab village founded in the 7th century that was ethnically cleansed of Palestinians by Israel in 1948. The archaeology of uncovering ancient Jewish artifacts turns reality upside-down: Palestinians are accused of occupying Jewish land.

I have not forgotten the question David asked thirty years ago about why there is a Holocaust Memorial in Boston (and 84 other U.S. cities). Now I understand it. What is Boston's relationship to the Holocaust? As a landscape architect, I know that addressing a site's context is the most important quality of a work. Did I over-look the Memorial's lack of a contextual relationship to the Holocaust and instead talk with my students about such architectural qualities as the transparency of the six engraved and lighted glass towers, the cleverness of the "smoke" that rises from the ground, and the experience of moving through it?

There are indeed Jews in Boston whose families suffered from the Holocaust, as there are in many places. I know some of them and they support Palestinian rights. But I am now suspicious, as David was long ago, of the big donors who brought that project forward. Furthermore, now a Holocaust Museum is being planned for Boston. Why would plans for a Holocaust Museum arise now? Both of these projects feel like what David has called "bullying." When will we be able to talk about what happened after the Holocaust? When will we be able to talk about anti-Palestinian hate?

Today I would ask another question of Boston: Why is the most iconic structure, the Zakim Bridge, in a city with a long history of famous people, named after a largely unknown person who led the ADL at the time when its policies were changing from protecting Jews to protecting Israel? One must wonder how the naming of that bridge came about. Rather than memorialize the ADL, I join with the people of Charlestown who prefer to call it the Bunker Hill Bridge. Plus, that name has a site-specific context: the battle of Bunker Hill actually took place on a hill that can be seen from the Bridge.

Most of all, Israel's war against Palestinians has undermined my country. The hypocrisy of U.S. bombs killing civilians and de-stroying homes, schools, universities and hospitals to "help Israel defend itself" is devastating. Our relationship with Israel has un-dermined our already vulnerable respect for democracy, human rights, and international law in the U.S. The International Court of Justice and, later, the International Criminal Court (ICC) were created to enforce the Geneva Convention standards clarifying war crimes. Since the ICC issued arrest warrants for Netanyahu for war crimes and directing attacks against the civilian population, Biden and Trump defended him.

The Nakba continues. But this war is very different from 1948. One person who experienced both describes their difference: the 1948 Israeli occupation of the land was carried out by soldiers, whereas in today's war, Israeli soldiers are nearly absent from battle. When we see photos of them, they are in small groups watching bombs explode (and often cheering), or simply arresting and shooting people. It is now a weapons-industry war carried out on screens with targeted U.S. bombs. Does the U.S. support international law only when it doesn't infringe upon our weapons sales?

It's unbelievable the spell that Zionists have put over Americans. They have deceived us over decades with prying solicitation, without any pretext of regret, grasping at military support for their hatred. The U.S. has given more monetary support to Israel—tiny, wealthy and technologically sophisticated—than any other country since WWII. Courageously, Representative Rashida Tlaib and Senator Bernie Sanders have recently been outspoken in their opposition to spending billions more taxpayer dollars on unconditional military aid to Israel. Supporting Israel's ethnic cleansing is clearly in violation of U.S. and international law. With strong support from a majority of Americans, in November, 2024, 19 U.S. Senators, including Warren and Markey from Massachusetts, voted to end illegal arms sales to Israel. Do the constituents of the other 81 Senators understand that they support illegal arms sales and genocide? When will the U.S. and Israel pay the price for denying international law?

Every day for more than a year I wake up and wonder how it could be possible that both parties in my country, Presidents Biden and now Trump, have supported such horrendous violence by giving the weapons industry tens of billions of taxpayer dollars to provide Israel with bombs to kill innocent children and civilians, and to destroy the homes, hospitals, and universities of an occupied people whose land has been taken from them?

Why is the medical community largely silent about the targeting of medical workers and the destruction of hospitals across Gaza?

Why is the educational community not only largely silent about the destruction of every university in Gaza and their loss to 90,000 students but also punishing their own students who speak the truth about this violence?

Why are climate activists largely silent on the environmental horrors of the weapons industry and, in particular, the most damaging of climate events, the release of carbon from bombing and the carbon costs of rebuilding?

When will we take responsibility for our support of daily violence against innocent civilians? It's not complicated. Genocide is always wrong. Negotiating justice is complicated. Young people understand that Palestine is a turning point upon which our failure to acknowledge the truth and end our violence will hollow their future. Will Israel have the grace of Germany to acknowledge its hatred and pay reparations?

www.ingramcontent.com/pod-product-compliance
Lightning Source LLC
Chambersburg PA
CBHW060358090426
42734CB00011B/2185